Queens
of Britain

Norah Lofts
Queens
of Britain

HODDER AND STOUGHTON
LONDON SYDNEY AUCKLAND TORONTO

This book was designed and produced by
George Rainbird Limited,
36 Park Street, London W1Y 4DE
for Hodder & Stoughton Ltd,
Mill Road, Dunton Green,
Sevenoaks, Kent

ISBN 0 340 21587 9

Text Filmset by Filmtype Services Limited, Scarborough

Printed and bound by Dai Nippon Printing Company
Limited, Tokyo, Japan

FRONTISPIECE
A portrait medallion of Margaret of Anjou
in 1463 by Piero da Milano.
Crown copyright, Victoria and Albert Museum, London

Contents

8

Introduction

I have been accused of over-emphasising the tragedy of Queens: but I am sure that if all the Queens the world has ever known could rise from their graves and give a truthful account of their lives the majority of their stories would be on the sorrowful side. Until very recently being female was in itself a disadvantage but Queens had extra miseries to bear.

How homesick most of them must have been, those young princesses, doomed to perpetual exile, to speak a foreign tongue, observe foreign fashions – even in dress – and all too often be regarded with dislike and suspicion. Well into the nineteenth century all royal marriages were arranged by people who believed – though it had been shown again and again to be a delusion – that the gift of a daughter could seal a treaty, placate an enemy, secure a friend . . . It was one of the silliest notions that ever contributed to the human predicament. Many fathers, in all other ways sensible, even shrewd, clung to the idea that a daughter, married to the King of Ruritania, would ensure friendship, or at least neutrality, from his son-in-law. Then would come a shift in politics, and there was the poor girl, Ruritanian in all but birth, cut off not only from her own people but from those of the country of which she was Queen. Then her own nationality would be held against her and she would be hissed in the streets.

This is not an imaginary situation. It happened all too often.

Then there was this business of child-bearing. Important to every woman, but immeasurably more so to a Queen. A man with an acre and an old donkey to bequeath wanted, needed, a son to inherit. How much more so a King with wide realms and high titles to pass on? Failure to produce a son, or any child at all, was for many centuries blamed upon the woman. Nobody took note of the fact that Eleanor of Aquitaine, Queen of England for many years, had formerly been married to the King of France and borne girls. He divorced her and she married Henry II and bore him four great troublesome boys.

For Queens also there was the pressure of the double standard. A King was allowed to take mistresses, bring them to Court, acknowledge and enoble their children. A Queen must be either chaste, very clever or very rash; for infidelity on her part was treason, and the penalty was severe. Two of Henry VIII's Queens ended on the block and, in comparatively civilized times, George IV's Queen had the doors of Westminster Abbey slammed in her face on what should have been her coronation day as well as his.

However, amongst the sad stories there are success stories . . .

Boadicea

Strictly speaking, Boadicea has no place here; she was not Queen of Britain, but she was British, and she was heroic, and she fought for a seemingly lost cause. She is remembered.

Her husband ruled a tribe called the Iceni which occupied part of Norfolk during the time of the Roman occupation; and he was – superficially at least – a friend of Rome, occupying much the same position as the Native Princes of India did under British rule. The Romans in Britain were perpetually undermanned and glad enough to let a friendly native rule his own tribe, provided that he adhered to certain laws and customs.

One pernicious custom that had grown up in the Roman Empire was that owners of land should will a good slice of their property to the Emperor. Boadicea's husband conformed and when he died in AD 60 left all his possessions to be divided between his two daughters and the Emperor Nero.

How fascinating to think of Nero, watching the games in the arena through his split-emerald eye-glass, being the owner of some land in Norfolk.

When Boadicea's husband died, the Emperor's agents moved in and demanded not the half, but the whole. Boadicea protested, and was beaten, her daughters were raped.

The Governor of what, to the Romans, was only a petty province, was Suetonius Paulinus, an honourable and able man; and he was busy elsewhere. Paulinus would be the first to spit upon the unctuous theory that he attacked the island of Anglesey, in the far west, in order to root out the native religion and do away with the Druids whose rites included human sacrifice. With what was going on in Rome at the time, gladiatorial contests to the death, the Christians to the lions, it is impossible to believe that a few Druids,

The statue of Queen Boadicea, on Westminster Bridge in London.

making a few human sacrifices, roused much revulsion in Paulinus or any other Roman. They wanted Anglesey because it was said to be rich in minerals, including silver.

With the Governor of Britain – and many of his men – thus engaged, Boadicea judged it time to lead a revolt. Other tribes joined the Iceni and they sacked Colchester, St Albans and London. They are said to have killed more than 70,000 Romans and pro-Romans and to have annihilated the famous Ninth Legion which came marching down from Lincoln.

Paulinus, as soon as the news of the uprising reached him, abandoned his metal search, rallied all Romans and defeated Boadicea and her undisciplined forces in one great battle – where is uncertain. Boadicea, in despair, poisoned herself. But she had made a point. Once the inevitable retaliation was over, Rome ruled with a kindlier hand.

Her name, spelt in various ways, is said to be the equivalent of Victoria; and it is interesting to think that though in the far future another Victoria was to have innumerable memorials erected in places the Romans never heard of, Boadicea's single memorial still stands in the London that she sacked.

Queens of Myth and Legend

The Romans withdrew from Britain in 426 and the remote, misty island sank into obscurity. The Angles, Jutes and Saxons who moved in, first to raid and then to settle, were not literate; they conveyed their stories by word of mouth, in songs called sagas – we still call a story that goes on and on, covering several generations, a saga. Stories thus transmitted cannot be constant in content; something may be omitted, and presently forgotten; something else added, and presently regarded as fact. And always to be remembered is the singer's need to please his audience, so the songs would be twisted. Some nub of truth might be there, growing more and more obscure under the accretion of myth and legend.

King Arthur and his beautiful but unfaithful Queen Guinivere belong to the lost years. Scholars now believe that Arthur did exist, a kind of knight errant, making a last-ditch stand against the encroaching barbarians; they believe that diligent digging may reveal the site of Camelot; but most of Arthur's story is unashamed romance, produced a thousand years later by Sir Thomas Malory and copied by Tennyson after another four centuries.

In the year 597 St Augustine brought Christianity and literacy to England; and in Kent there was a Queen who deserves mention. Her name was Bertha and she encouraged the new religion and persuaded her husband to give Augustine and his forty monk companions a residence at Canterbury.

Within a hundred years there were many such religious establishments, and in them monks, writing in Latin. One of them, the Venerable Bede, in the seventh century, wrote a massive history, which King Alfred the Great, good scholar as well as good soldier, translated.

History written by cloistered monks was as slanted as history sung to please an all male audience; neither way were women much regarded except as good wives, good mothers or as good patrons of the Church.

Guinivere by William Morris

*I thought I could not breathe in that fine air, that pure severity of perfect
Light – I wanted warmth and colour which I found in Lancelot – now I see
Thee what thou art, thou art the highest and most human too, not
Lancelot, nor another. Is there none will tell the King I love him tho'
So late?*

*A tenth-century ivory tablet depicting monks busy at their
writing labours.*

Until the Norman Conquest in 1066 – the one date that everyone knows –
even the use of the word *Queen* is of dubious value; the ruler's wife was
known as his Lady, or as his Companion. William the Conqueror's wife,
Matilda, was the first woman to whom the title of *Regina* was ever accorded.

Matilda

Queen to William the Conqueror
born about 1031, married 1053, died 1083

Matilda was extremely well-connected, daughter of the Earl of Flanders and counting amongst her ancestors highly-born people of French, English, German and even some Norman blood, a fact which caused a little trouble when William chose her for his wife.

[handwritten margin note: Good family]

She was well-educated and said to be beautiful – though modern research shows that she escaped being a dwarf only by an inch or two. Her father had no wish to see her married to William, who was a bastard and whose claim to the Dukedom of Normandy was dubious in the extreme. Moreover, they were cousins and the Church disapproved of consanguineous marriages. And Matilda had already fallen in love with a young Englishman who had come on a diplomatic mission to her father's Court.

[handwritten margin note: very short]

However, William was a man who liked his own way, and, peaceful approaches having failed, resorted to violence; he set about Matilda one morning as she emerged from church, tore her rich clothing, flung her down in the street and gave her several slaps for good measure. He did not abduct her; he rode away. At the time of the assault she was about sixteen years old and he was twenty. They were both five years older when they were married, with great pomp. (What would one not give for a frank, first-hand account of her thoughts and feelings during that time? The fair-haired young Englishman was still alive – heading towards an unenviable fate. And why should her father have changed from opposition to a state in which 'he gave Matilda joyfully'? It was not that William's position had improved; it had seldom been worse; he had many enemies, some of them within his own dukedom.)

Married they were and the Pope showed his displeasure at this marriage of cousins by excommunicating them both. Then he relented – on conditions. Both were to erect a religious house. William built St Stephen's Abbey for monks; Matilda built the Abbaye-aux-Dames at Caen for nuns.

*The Abbey built by Matilda in Normandy to honour her
marriage vows.*

Building the ships for the Norman invasion, from the Bayeux Tapestry.

The marriage appears to have been happy; Matilda bore in all four sons and six daughters; and when in 1066, William set out on his great enterprise, the conquest of England, he left his wife in charge of Normandy. In return for this gesture of confidence, Matilda had built and fitted out a secret ship to add to William's gathering navy. She had spared no expense; the figure-head was either of gold or gilded bronze; an effigy of their youngest son, holding in one hand a bow, its arrow aimed towards England, and in the other a trumpet. William took it as his flag-ship.

Matilda first set foot in England in April 1068 and was crowned at Winchester on Whit Sunday of that year. William had been crowned already, but he shared her coronation in order to make the occasion more splendid. She was the first real Queen of England.

By this time the fair-haired young Englishman who had attracted her girlish favour was deep in a dungeon from which he was never to emerge alive. Some slight mystery surrounds his horrible fate. Certainly a good many Englishmen who refused to acknowledge William were incarcerated for a time, certainly most English estates were confiscated. But except when faced with direct defiance, William followed a policy of conciliation. His treatment of Brihtric, not, so far as is known, a rebel, was unusually severe and is sometimes attributed to retrospective jealousy. Another theory holds that although Matilda had fallen in love with Brihtric, he had slighted her and she was now taking revenge. Possibly the truth of this will never be known.

Matilda's name is irrevocably associated with the Bayeux Tapestry – which is not a tapestry at all but a colossal piece of embroidery nearly twenty inches wide and seventy-seven yards long. Matilda and her ladies may have

*Matilda's 'mark' next to that of her husband on a charter drawn
up between 1072 and 1076.*

plied their needles upon it, but experts now doubt that it is, as it has for long
been considered, all their own work. One most interesting thing about it
is that the pictures are said to have been designed by a dwarf. And it is a
fact that Matilda's favourite son was known by the nickname, 'Curthose',
meaning, roughly, short-legged. It could be a case of a very small woman,
a near-dwarf, liking people who did not make her feel small.

Her favouritism for Robert Curthose clouded her last years. Encouraged
by her he rebelled against his father, and although there was a reconciliation,
there were other rebellions, too.

Two of her daughters were already dead and she fell into a state of ill-
health, depression and – in the fashion of the day – religious fervour. She
died in Normandy when she was fifty-one, and William who was in
England hastened to her bedside. After her death he was so grieved that,
much as he loved hunting, he forswore it.

She may have been his talisman. Certainly in the four years of his widowhood his luck seemed to desert him and he died, in great pain, 'without a
friend or kinsman near his bed'.

Matilda of Scotland

First Queen to Henry I
born 1080, married 1100, died 1118

At the time of the Conquest there was, living in England a young man, Edgar the Atheling who had a better claim to the English crown than either of the men who had fought for it at Hastings. He could trace a blood kinship back to Alfred the Great. William the Conqueror treated him and his family well – part of his conciliation policy – but in 1068, Edgar became suspicious of William's ultimate intentions and, with his mother and two sisters, took ship for the Continent, hoping to get to Hungary where they had relatives.

Bad weather drove their ship to the coast of Scotland where Malcolm Canmore had just taken the crown from Macbeth. The King of Scotland received the fugitives kindly and fell in love with Margaret, Edgar's older sister. He married her. One of their children was a girl, given the old English name of Edith, or Editha, and some authorities say that she had a second name, Matilda.

There followed some muddling wars and presently Edith found herself back in England, a girl without a father, placed in the care of her aunt, the Abbess of Romsey.

The Abbess believed – and her own position must have confirmed her belief – that both warfare and politics stopped short at the convent door; therefore the only safe place for a girl was a convent. She did her best to persuade Edith to take the veil and become a professed nun. It is said that the Abbess actually put the veil over Edith's head and that the girl took it off, and behind her aunt's back, stamped upon it. Occasionally, when an unwanted suitor arrived, she wore it willingly; and between putting it on and throwing it off, she acquired the kind of education which in that age

Matilda depicted in the Golden Book of St Albans.

only a convent could supply. Her learning and her love of music made her a most suitable wife for the Conqueror's fourth son, Henry the Good Scholar.

Henry had been free to follow his scholarly preoccupations for his chances of being either Duke of Normandy or King of England were negligible while his brothers lived.

One of his brothers was dead – killed in a hunting accident in the ill-fated New Forest – and in the year 1100 William II – to whom the Conqueror had bequeathed England – was killed in that same forest, in more mysterious circumstances. William left no heir. Henry was King and he hastened to ingratiate himself as far as possible with the native English and the pro-English Normans.

He married Edith, who either took or reverted to the more Norman name of Matilda and then became known as Good Queen Maud.

The Church put up some opposition to the marriage, claiming that Edith-Matilda was a professed nun – it is from this objection that we learn the details of that veil rejected, accepted when convenient, rejected again. The Council called to inquire into the situation declared her free to marry.

With her learning, her piety and her good practical sense she made an excellent Queen, encouraging Henry in his liberal policies towards the English.

She was a friend to many religious houses, and would on occasion give proof of humility by washing – and kissing – the feet of beggars. Her courtiers thought this a deplorable practice and begged her 'for Godde's love' to desist.

One of her worldly interests was in means of communication; she encouraged the restoration of the old roads that the Romans had left, and the making of new ones. The first arched bridge in England was built under her patronage, and was called a bow bridge. It gave Stratford-le-Bow its name.

Henry and Matilda had two children, a son named William for his grand-father and a daughter named Matilda who made a grand marriage and became Empress. (The Empire of early and medieval times is difficult to define – its borders could expand or contract. It consisted of a loose con-federation of kingdoms, duchies and principalities occupying much of Europe and headed by an Emperor who was *elected*.)

Henry I had not been reared to war and was not, like his father, a con-spicuously good soldier, but wars were forced upon him and whenever he was forced to go abroad to fight against his own brother, Robert, Duke of Normandy, or against the King of France, he paid Matilda the compliment which his father had paid *his* Queen – leaving her in charge of the country.

But she died before him and he showed his respect and affection for her by confirming all her gifts and continuing to support all her charities. By dying in 1118 she escaped the tragic grief of knowing that her only son was dead, not in battle, not of disease but in the wreck of the ship in which he had been returning to England, a disaster largely due to the Prince's generosity with wine to the crew.

Some records say that Matilda lies buried in Westminster Abbey, near to her uncle, Edward the Confessor; but the monks at Reading claimed that she was buried in their Abbey; Winchester is named as her burial place too. The confusion probably arose because so many memorials were erected to her memory. Good Queen Maud was greatly loved.

Adelicia

Second Queen to Henry I
born 1103, married 1121, died 1151

Henry's grief for Queen Maud, genuine as it seems to have been, did not prevent him from marrying again shortly after her death. This was a year after the shipwreck in which his heir died, so the begetting of another son was a matter of immediate urgency. Also he probably missed his wife and her support and companionship; if so, he chose a rather curious replacement. Adelicia was only eighteen, said to have been of remarkable beauty but only of mediocre education.

However, Henry was so eager to marry her that he did not haggle over her dowry; her father was astonished at the magnanimity of the King of England.

Before the century was out, Henry's grandson, another Henry, was engaged in that hand-to-hand struggle with the Church which culminated in Thomas-à-Becket's death; and that the Church needed some curbing is proved by the almost incredible behaviour of an archbishop and a bishop over the marriage and the coronation, which were to take place at Windsor and at Westminster on successive days. The Bishop of Salisbury claimed the right to perform both ceremonies because Windsor was within his diocese; the Archbishop of Canterbury, though of great age, and partially paralysed, disputed this and called a Council to decide the matter. The Council's verdict was that wherever the King and Queen were, within the boundaries of England, they were parishioners of the Archbishop of Canterbury. So he performed the first ceremony, and he was so slow and tottering that Henry decided to entrust next day's ceremony to the Bishop of Salisbury, who was, in any case his favourite.

Henry had been crowned on his accession, but intended to be crowned again as a compliment to his bride. The crown had actually been placed on his head by the Bishop when the Archbishop arrived and angrily asked the King who had put the crown on his head. The more dramatic chroniclers state that the Archbishop knocked the crown off with a blow from his

*Adelicia of Louvain would have been dressed
very like the woman in this manuscript illumination.*

crozier; others say he removed it. He then performed the whole ceremony
again, and proceeded to crown the young Queen.

Despite her youth, Adelicia did her best to share Henry's interests while
they were together – which was seldom; and when he was absent behaved
in an impeccable manner. He cannot have been a very cheerful companion
after his son was drowned; he is said never to have smiled again.

Perhaps he might have mustered a smile had Adelicia produced a son,
but she did not, and when Henry was fifty-eight he apparently gave up all

hope, and began to make plans for his daughter, the Empress, to succeed him. She was already, at twenty-four, a widow.

The English and the Anglo-Norman faction agreed readily to accept her – she was the daughter of Good Queen Maud; the Normans gave more consideration to the Salic Law which prevented females from inheritance. Henry used persuasion, he was prepared to buy oaths of allegiance to his daughter. He arranged a new marriage for her – to the son of the powerful Duke of Anjou – and, although she had borne the Emperor no child, by Geoffrey of Anjou she had a son.

And all the time, visiting England often, being affable and charming and dispensing lavish hospitality, was the man who was to ruin Henry's plans. His name was Stephen, and he was the son of one of William the Conqueror's daughters – so he was Henry's nephew and the Empress Matilda's cousin. Henry I had shown him many favours, and of all those who owed allegiance to Henry and were prepared to swear allegiance to the Empress, Stephen was the second to do so – preceded only by the King of Scotland. Stephen took an oath which he had not the slightest intention to keep.

Henry I died in Normandy in the year 1135 when he was sixty-six and his Queen only thirty-two. Adelicia had always behaved as a Queen should, and she behaved as royal widows were expected to do. She was well-to-do, for Henry had dowered her richly; she gave manors to religious houses to secure Masses to be said for his soul, and – imaginative touch – out of her income from the wharf in London known as Queenhythe, she provided funds to pay for an oil-lamp to burn perpetually before his tomb. (A hundred shillings was a vast sum in those days, but the only lamp-oil was olive, brought from southern Europe and very expensive.)

After a year of mourning spent in the convent of Wilton, Adelicia emerged and married William de Albini, the son of one of the knights who had come over with the Conqueror and received a good slice of Norfolk land as a reward. William de Albini was a man of the highest reputation. One of Adelicia's dowers was Arundel Castle – and by this marriage began the association of the Dukes of Norfolk with Arundel.

To Henry Adelicia had given no child. To her second husband she bore a number of children, seven of whom survived. They all made good marriages, and took the blood of a Queen of England into many families of the English aristocracy.

Two of her blood-kin left a mark on history; two Queens, both unfortunate, Anne Boleyn and Catherine Howard, were related to the Duke of Norfolk.

After eleven years of an apparently happy marriage, Adelicia, with the full consent of her husband, withdrew from the world and retired to a convent in Flanders. It may have been a retreat from an awkward situation.

*Even the remains of Arundel Castle are enough to explain why
a gentle person like Adelicia might prefer to end her days in a convent.*

Adelicia must have known – better than anyone – how very anxious Henry I had been to see his daughter succeed to his throne and what faith he had placed in the oath sworn by his barons, especially by his nephew Stephen. Yet the King was hardly buried before Stephen, backed by other oath-takers who disliked the idea of a woman on the throne, and by a strong force of mercenaries, had himself proclaimed King. That was the beginning of a civil war in which it was difficult for Adelicia to remain neutral. The Empress Matilda, coming to assert *her* claim, went straight to Arundel Castle; Adelicia could hardly be expected to turn her step-daughter away. For the next eight years the war went on. Adelicia is described as a gentle person and England during those years was no place for a gentle person, far less one more or less committed. One understands her husband giving his full consent to her withdrawal.

And it is impossible not to think that Adelicia, looking around at the confusion, the cruelty and the lawlessness, did not think that if she had managed to give Henry just *one* of the sons she had given her second husband, all this could have been avoided.

The Empress Matilda

Lady of the English
born 1102, married 1128, died 1164

The most fascinating word in history is *if* . . .

If the Empress Matilda had come to the throne, as her father intended . . . If Stephen had not forestalled her . . .

Matilda was the Conqueror's granddaughter and she had inherited something of his character. People who disliked her called her proud and arrogant – but the great barons of England, and the princes of the church were proud and arrogant themselves and needed curbing. She would probably have done better than Stephen who was so affable and agreeable.

In a way she was a strategist. She did not attack the usurper at once. She waited for Stephen to outlive his first popularity.

Some of his rulings, aimed to please everybody, pleased nobody. The one regarding hunting is a good example. The Conqueror had imposed some savage laws for the protection of game; Stephen revoked the laws; anybody could hunt anything, anywhere, and within a year there was almost nothing for anybody to hunt. Stephen was then obliged to re-impose the laws – about the worst thing, from the point of popularity, that any ruler can do.

Stephen had also fallen out with the Church.

Matilda judged that the moment had come. She brought no army with her, she felt that she could rely upon Stephen's enemies for all the support she needed. Up to a point she was right. Even the City of London, after only the briefest hesitation, opened the gates to her. And there had long been an adage – he who holds London, holds England.

She might have held it, had her manner been less haughty and her demands for money less burdensome. She was dealing, in London, with an element unfamiliar to her; not the great lord with thousands of acres and many sub-tenants upon whom any new imposition from above could

On her seal Matilda called herself Empress, by the Grace of God.
She also issued coins.

be in turn imposed, but with numerous comparatively small men who, when they paid taxes, paid them out of their own earnings. This they resented.

Matilda's 'reign' lasted only eight months; she was never in a position secure enough to impose her will upon the whole country. Although she was crowned she did not call herself Queen of England; she was the Empress and Lady of the English; the latter title with its historic links being perhaps a sop to English feeling, but the sequence was ill-chosen.

The see-saw of civil war swung on, doing endless damage, less from the direct confrontation of armed forces than from the breakdown of law and order which allowed the strong to rob and exploit the weak. Agriculture declined and the roads in which Henry I's first wife had taken such interest fell into disuse since they were so infested by robbers.

*An enamel plaque showing Geoffrey Plantagenet, Matilda's
second husband. It is the first record of a shield of arms.*

The contest, which was socially and economically so ruinous, ended in
deadlock. Stephen was to reign for the rest of his life and then the throne
was to pass to Matilda's son by her second husband, Henry Plantagenet,
who had already proved his ability as a soldier.

Some chroniclers hint that there had once been more than a cousinly
relationship between Matilda and Stephen and that Henry was Stephen's
child. It may have been mere gossip; writers who worked in cloistered
seclusion must have been dangerously dependent upon hearsay. There was
nothing of Stephen in Henry's make-up; and very little of the man who was
his legal father. He was much more like his great-grandfather, the Conqueror.
Presently England was to feel the weight – and the healing – of his rule.

Matilda of Boulogne

Queen to Stephen
born about 1103, married by 1125, died 1152

Matilda is rather difficult to place – even chronologically. Certainly she was
crowned in England before the Empress Matilda, but a good many people
always regarded the Empress as the rightful heir and Stephen as the usurper,
and during Matilda's brief reign, this other Matilda could hardly regard
herself as Queen.

Her lineage is clear; she was a granddaughter of the Conqueror and
therefore cousin of Stephen and to the Empress; but of her early life little
is known. It is supposed that she received the usual conventual education
in the convent of Bermondsey. Then, given the necessary dispensation for
marriage between first cousins – seldom refused where high rank was
involved – she married Stephen of Blois and proved to be a good wife to
a bad husband.

Stephen was handsome and charming and completely unreliable, as
unfaithful to his marriage vows as he was to his oath to accept the Empress
Matilda as his overlord. But that was no unusual situation and Matilda
appears to have accepted it calmly.

While Henry I lived, the young couple spent a good deal of their time
in England; the King built them a palace and called it Tower Royal; both
children born early in their marriage died young and were buried in London.

How much did Matilda know of Stephen's ultimate intentions? And
how much of that reputedly violent love affair which he had had with the
Empress Matilda? We can never know. There are a few clues; all the time
when Stephen was in London, being affable to all and sundry – rather like
a candidate for election – Matilda was by his side, being charming, and
being English. Speaking English, which at a time when the two languages,
English and Norman-French, were melding together must have pleased a
good many people who were slightly behind the times.

Matilda was heavily pregnant when Stephen took the throne upon Henry's death and she could not share his coronation on St Stephen's day, in the dead winter of 1135. Her child was born, a boy, and by Easter Sunday of the next year she was crowned.

Like most of the best philanderers, Stephen in public honoured his wife and he gave her a grand coronation which he could well afford, for the civil war which was to bring such ruin had not begun then, and he had his uncle, Henry I's treasury to draw upon.

Any honour or affection which Stephen showed his Queen, she more than amply repaid when, later on, with the Empress in the ascendant, Stephen lay in Bristol gaol. His wife did her best, by personal petition, by trying to arrange an exchange of prisoners and finally by an attack upon the Empress, to secure his release.

She did not live to see the peace arranged. Since it ignored any rights which her own son, Eustace, had to the throne, it would hardly have pleased her. She died of one of those vague fevers so prevalent in times of poor sanitation and was buried in an abbey which she had helped to found. Its most cherished relic – presented by her – was a fragment of wood, said to be part of the True Cross. Such relics were not rare, but this was at the time of the Christian control of the Holy Land, and one of Matilda's uncles had been King of Jerusalem, so it is just possible that this one had more authenticity than most.

Matilda – of whom no representation or portrait seems to exist –
would have had candlesticks like this one in her palaces.

Eleanor of Aquitaine

Queen to Henry II
born 1122, married 1152, died 1204

Eleanor was the greatest heiress in Europe; with complete disregard of the Salic Law, the nobles of Aquitaine had sworn to acknowledge her as their Duchess.

She was beautiful. It is a conventional rule that all ladies of high rank should be described as beautiful, or at least pretty; Eleanor of Aquitaine was beautiful, with that beauty which youth can enhance, and even age can not destroy.

She had many suitors, but sensibly chose no one of them of whom the others could rightly be jealous. She married the King of France, Louis VII. Politically a wise choice but not one calculated to lead to a happy marriage. He was very pious; contemporaries said of him that he would have made a good monk; but he was a King and he was persuaded that it was his duty to go on a Crusade to liberate the Holy Land from the Saracens. It had been liberated before and a Christian Kingdom established there. The King of Jerusalem, now under renewed threat, was in fact Eleanor's uncle.

She insisted upon going on this Crusade and raised a company of women to join her – most of them women of property; for although the feudal system operated strongly against women there were gaps in the net. A fond father, a doting husband, even a loving brother could so arrange things that a woman could enjoy some independence. From such fortunate women, Eleanor recruited what was called the Queen's Guard.

This, the Second Crusade, was a muddle and a failure; but two small things show how fascinating Eleanor could be. Her uncle flirted with her, to put it mildly, and a young Saracen Emir, very handsome and wealthy, expressed a desire to marry her.

She came home in a cloud of disgrace. Louis considered divorcing her but was dissuaded by his clerical advisers, and possibly, if only slightly, by the thought that Aquitaine was a very rich province indeed.

When divorce was next mentioned, it was Eleanor who spoke the word. With all the force of her violent and romantic nature she had fallen in love with Henry Fitz-Empress, Henry Plantagenet; one day to be King of England.

He was her junior by twelve years, but he fell in love with her and although their marriage was turbulent, even by the standard of the time, it began well.

Eleanor asked the Church for an annulment of her marriage to the King of France, on the grounds that they were fourth cousins. Louis did not put up any opposition – she had borne him only two daughters and she was anything but a comfortable spouse. She had brought with her from the South some new and strange ideas about love, quite disconnected from matrimony, affairs almost of the imagination, to be expressed in songs and poems. She was elegant and sophisticated and learned – but not in Louis' own rather monkish way.

Henry and Eleanor were married at Bordeaux six weeks after the divorce had been granted; such haste was considered indecent, but she was a great heiress and beautiful and in that short interval two men – one of them Henry's younger brother – had attempted to abduct her. There was another reason for haste; the bride was five months pregnant. The King of France must have known that the child was not his.

The marriage made Henry master of most of what today is called France; he was Duke of Normandy, by arrangement with Stephen; Count of Anjou, by inheritance, and now Lord of Aquitaine. Within two years he was to be King of England, ruling a realm 'wider than Charlemagne's', but it was upon these wide domains and the question of which son should have which that trouble in the future was rooted.

Their first son, William, was born in Normandy and was brought to England as an infant when Stephen died.

Henry and Eleanor were crowned in Westminster Abbey with more magnificence than that building, already ageing, had ever seen; silks and brocades and gauze. The Crusade to which Eleanor had ridden was a failure in itself, but it had brought her in touch with the magnificence of the East; into her own province of Aquitaine she had introduced silk worms and the white mulberry trees on whose leaves they lived. She loved jewellery and possessed a good deal of it. Her veils, more decorative than concealing, were held in place by jewelled circlets, even the collars of her dresses gleamed with precious stones.

It was strange that so much grandeur – even clergymen wore for the first time in England magnificent robes of silk and velvet – should be introduced into a country which civil war and maladministration had rendered so poor. The new, unlicensed castles were no more than robbers' strongholds; who was going to be industrious and thrifty when the result would be stolen? There were authenticated cases where a man merely suspected of having a little wealth was taken and tortured until he told where it was, or – having none – died.

With his passion for law and order and his superhuman energy, Henry II was just the man to tackle the job of setting things to rights.

He started on the eleven hundred illicit castles; 'Show your licence or pull it down!' He divided the whole country into regions, each to be visited regularly by a judge appointed by himself, charged to see that the King's peace was kept and the King's justice done. It was said that soon after his accession a virgin could walk from one end of his realm to another with her bosom full of gold and suffer no harm. His quarrel with Thomas-à-Becket – once his dear friend – was over a matter of simple justice; Becket held that any cleric – and he gave the word its widest interpretation – should be above the law while Henry believed that everybody should be subject to it.

Eleanor's love of luxurious objects extended to her present-
giving. She gave this crystal vase to Louis VII, King of France,
her first husband.
Eleanor, serene at last, may still be seen lying in effigy at
Fontevrault Abbey.

He managed to do so much during relatively short visits to England, for he had his other domains to see to and little wars to wage, partly by cutting down on meal-times – he could eat his dinner standing up, in five minutes.

He also made time for amorous ventures. The one in which Eleanor was most concerned is the often told and generally garbled affair of Rosamond Clifford, who had been his mistress before his marriage and continued to be so for a time afterwards.

The stories – quite fascinating – about Eleanor tracking down her rival by means of a reel of silk thread and then disposing of her by stabbing or poisoning, can hardly stand up against the fact that Rosamond died twenty years after her reputed murder, in a nunnery at Godstow. The proliferation of the legends and ballads proves that on the whole Eleanor was not popular except with those who came into contact with her and the growing middle class; some London merchants were making fortunes out of the wine trade with Aquitaine and the import of silk. She was foreign; English and Norman blood were slowly intermingling and Henry always emphasised his Englishry. Eleanor had none.

Much of her time and energy was for some years devoted to child-bearing. Young William, whose date of birth had caused so much scandal, died and was buried near his great-grandfather, Henry I. But there was a daughter, Matilda, and Henry and Richard and Geoffrey and John and Eleanor and Joanna.

Grand, politically-orientated and sometimes very consanguineous marriages were planned for all these children almost from birth. Matilda was to marry a French prince and Richard a French princess; and Joanna the King of Sicily. Geoffrey was betrothed to Constance of Brittany and Eleanor to the King of Castile – a fact which gave a later Plantagenet a reason for putting forward a claim to the throne of that country.

Disguise it however cleverly, most parents have a favourite among their children. Henry's favourite was John, his last-born son; Eleanor's was Richard. He was, to her and to generations of people long afterwards, the perfect knight; handsome, outstandingly brave, adept at all feats of arms, but not the mere war-machine which was the Norman ideal. He was a maker and a singer of songs. The romantic South was in his blood and Aquitaine must be his.

Henry would probably have preferred to see his favourite, John, become King of England, but Henry was the elder and must succeed, so, to ensure the succession, he had him crowned, as the Young King in his own life-time, a gesture which evoked neither loyalty nor gratitude from the son. All Eleanor's sons were in an almost constant state of rebellion against their father, and Eleanor encouraged them.

Why?

The King's infidelities must have been irksome to a proud woman and one of his affairs was particularly shocking even in an age not easily shocked. Alys, the Princess of France, betrothed to Richard and sent to the English Court to learn English language and customs, was seduced by Richard's father.

The gap of twelve years in age, which had seemed nothing when Henry, Duke of Normandy fell in love with the Queen of France, widened as the years advanced. The union which had begun so romantically and been so fruitful declined into sordid squabbling and so many conspiracies against Henry that finally he decided that it was no longer safe to allow his wife to be at large. He consigned her to a mild form of imprisonment, what we would call 'house arrest', in Winchester.

She was brought out from time to time, put on show for family or political reasons; but always returned to Winchester where she was housed as comfortably as she would have been in any other English royal residence; but she was cut off from the world and from the busy little conspiracies which had been her main interest. Her imprisonment is described as 'mysterious', and it is a mystery why she should have submitted to it. She had shown herself on more than one occasion to be physically fearless and she was not without resources. Even more of a mystery is that she emerged at the end of sixteen years apparently undamaged, ready to resume life, take up responsibility, wield influence, as she did in 1189, when Henry died and Richard became King of England. The Young King had died six years earlier.

Overnight her position was changed from that of prisoner whose every word and action was under strict surveillance, to that of being, after the King, the first power in the land; often, since he was frequently absent, *the* first power. And this at the age of sixty-seven.

Richard needed – and she realised it – every bit of help and good counsel that he could obtain. He was not then popular in England, he had spent too much time in Aquitaine. He did not even speak English well. One of Eleanor's first acts was to order a general gaol opening. She knew how hateful imprisonment could be and she knew how the prisoners, many of them awaiting trial or being punished for some infringement of the savage forest laws, would go about praising this act of clemency ordered in the name of the new King.

She pleased the religious houses too by removing an irksome burden which Henry had imposed upon them. Because Henry's journeys about England had always been made at top speed, and at unpredictable times, he needed horses kept at places not too far apart, all over the country, and kept in tip-top condition. Since inns were few and unreliable, Henry stabled his horses at religious houses and while the burden bore lightly upon great rich abbeys, others found it heavy. Eleanor freed them of it.

In fact the new King was not going to need relays of horses on which to gallop about England; he was going on Crusade as soon as he had enough money. Eleanor knew from first-hand experience that crusading could be a dangerous business; she wanted to see Richard married, a prospective father before the Third Crusade began. Alys, though still unmarried, was out of the question, but far away in Navarre there was a princess of fabulous beauty who was reputed to have fallen in love with Richard when he visited her father's Court for a tournament. Perhaps a marriage could be arranged...

It was arranged, largely through the efforts of Eleanor, elderly even by modern standards. Since Richard had no time for wooing, must be off on Crusade at the first possible moment, it was his mother who made the long journey to the little country which lay just south of the Pyrenees, took charge of the necessary negotiations and conducted the bride-to-be to Sicily, the rendezvous.

She did not see her favourite son married, nor follow, as she intended to do, this Crusade. The people to whom the government of England had been entrusted – one of them her youngest son, John – were behaving treacherously. So, after only four days' rest, off again.

She governed England, wisely and well, calling herself, and signing herself, Queen of England, though Richard's marriage to Berengaria had actually relegated her to the status of Queen Mother, and the years were mounting.

She lived to hear how Richard, within sight of Jerusalem, was let down by his fellow Crusaders; and then, on his way back to England, taken and imprisoned, held for some extortionate ransom. She busied herself with the raising of it, saw him freed, saw him re-crowned – a rite needed to remove the dishonour of imprisonment. She had a brief time of great glory, travelling with Richard as he went about showing himself to the people who could forgive what he had cost them – a quarter of every man's income for a year – because he was already a legend in his life-time; the best warrior in the world; one who, but for treachery, would have saved Jerusalem. Wherever he went, Eleanor went too; at feasts and public gatherings she always had the place of honour at his right hand.

Did it worry her then, that, though married, he was childless; had never even bothered to bring his Queen to England? Perhaps she was beyond worrying about a state of affairs which she could not alter?

She outlived her favourite son by five years. Back in her own sunny Aquitaine, she remained busy and active and intelligent – if Constance of Brittany had taken her advice her son, Arthur might have been more fortunate than he was. One of the marriages which Eleanor arranged in her last years was that of her granddaughter, Blanche of Castile, to the grandson of Louis VII. She lived to be eighty-two, a good age even now, and extraordinary in her time. It was almost as though Fate tried to repay all those wasted years at Winchester...

Berengaria of Navarre

Queen to Richard I
born 1165, married 1191, died about 1230

See colour plate facing page 64.

Berengaria was said to be the most beautiful woman of her generation; and her story proves, beyond doubt, that she was devoted to Richard Plantagenet. Both beauty and devotion were wasted. Richard, the best fighting man in Christendom, was a homosexual. (Twenty years ago the merest hint of this truth caused a great deal of shock and disbelief; now it is taken for granted.)

It may have been that when Berengaria looked down from the ladies' gallery upon the knights gathered for a tournament in her father's capital of Pamplona, she fell in love with a normal man. For Richard to discover that his own father had seduced the young Alys of France could have been a traumatic experience which, allied to an inherited trait, turned him against all women, except his mother.

Eleanor escorted Berengaria to Sicily, and then hurried away to save England, leaving Berengaria in the care of Richard's sister, Joanna. Richard rushed off to Cyprus, whose ruler proved to be unfriendly. Richard, his Crusaders and a number of discontented Cypriots, soon took Limasol, and there Richard and Berengaria were married and Berengaria was crowned Queen of England and of Cyprus. Then Richard hurried on to the Holy Land, and Berengaria followed. She and Joanna stayed in Acre while this Crusade – doomed from the first by divisions between the Christian forces – was fought and lost.

At the end of it, Richard saw his sister and his wife on to a ship westward bound, and then took what he believed to be a quicker route, overland. He was captured by a man with whom he had quarrelled bitterly during the Crusade, and for a long time even his whereabouts were unknown.

Berengaria got as far as Aquitaine, and there stayed. Why she did not complete her journey to England we are not told. Perhaps she felt safer in

The sculptor who wrought Berengaria's tomb in the Abbey of L'Epau has transmitted her beauty for us in stone.

Aquitaine than she would have done in England where John was going about saying that Richard was dead and asserting his right to the throne.

Then Richard's place of imprisonment was discovered and negotiations for ransoming him were begun.

The ransom demanded was extortionate; 150,000 marks. The mark was a measure of value, not a coin; it is sometimes said to have been worth a third of a pound – but the pound had worth in the twelfth century. To get this ransom together every man in England gave a fourth of his income, every sheep was shorn and its fleece sold, church plate was pawned. Most of the sacrifices were made gladly, for Richard was already a legendary figure – the man who, had he not been let down by faithless allies, would have freed the Holy Places from the Infidel.

Berengaria, in Aquitaine, helped to raise the ransom money. Richard came home to England, from which he had been absent, in all, four years; and was re-crowned to remove the shame of having been in prison. It would have seemed to any ordinary person an excellent opportunity to bring home his bride and present her to his people.

By this time the truth of the situation would have dawned on the most obtuse of women. Richard's way of life was being openly criticised and he was repeatedly being urged to live with his 'virtuous Queen'. Berengaria was in a humiliating situation, but she preserved her dignity and waited to be sent for. Her patience was rewarded when Richard fell ill and thought he was about to die. He then confessed his faults and vowed that if he recovered, and if Berengaria would forgive him, he would never forsake her again. He was on the Continent again by this time pursuing the endless war, and they met, were reconciled, kept Christmas of 1196 together and after that were never apart for long. But there was no child.

Richard suggested adopting his nephew, a boy called Arthur, the son of his dead brother Geoffrey; but the boy's mother, Constance, hated Eleanor who advised her to accept the offer, so she refused – a fatal decision.

Richard never returned to England – his continental possessions had always meant more to him than England which he looked upon as source of men and money for his wars; so Berengaria remained Queen of a country which she had never seen.

It is ironic that Richard, so nearly the perfect knight and certainly the best Crusader of his age, should have met his death through a sordid squabble about a non-existent treasure. On a field belonging to one of his vassals a ploughman turned up a pot containing some Roman coins. By the time word reached Richard, this modest find had been exaggerated into a number of golden statues and a bowlful of diamonds, which Richard, as overlord, demanded. Told that there was no such treasure, Richard besieged the castle of the man upon whose domain the riches were said to have been found; and an arrow from the battlements went through his shoulder.

Surgeons who pursued this trade alongside being blacksmiths or butchers, hacked the barbed arrow head out; the wound inflamed. The besieged castle had been captured and the man who had shot that arrow was brought into the room where Richard was dying in agony. Asked what should be done with the man, Richard said, 'Set him free'. That order was part of the magnanimity which was one facet of Richard's complicated character.

Berengaria was with him when he died – and she may have heard the screams when, contrary to the King's order, the man was lynched. She was a witness to the fact that Richard left his crown and his kingdom to his brother John, whose treachery while he was on Crusade he had forgiven with the same magnanimity.

She was well endowed; Richard had conferred upon her revenues derived from the tin and lead mines in Cornwall; on the Continent she owned the city of Le Mans and the county of Bigorre. She was still young and beautiful, but she never re-married. She went, as so many wealthy widows did, into a convent and devoted her life and her income to charitable works.

Berengaria had never been insistent upon her marital rights; about her financial ones she was very firm. John tried to shuffle out of paying her her English dues and finally she appealed to the Pope who was, at the time, contemplating excommunicating John; the wrongs suffered by Berengaria may have contributed to the final nudge.

Being charitable – and there was room for charity in those days – Berengaria outlived John and had a similar difficulty in getting her money from England after his death. But from this source and that she managed to get enough to feed beggars, care for abandoned children and build a stately abbey at L'Epau. There, having reached a fair age she died and was buried.

Why did she choose not to lay her bones beside those of Richard and his mother at Fontevrault? There is no answer to that question. The circumstances, and even the date of her death are uncertain. 'Old men forget', so do old women, and she may have outlived that long infatuation and have preferred to lie in death, as so often in life, alone.

Isabella
of Angoulême

Queen to John
born 1186, married 1200, died 1246

John, as a fourth son, with three healthy brothers, had never expected much in the way of territory. In his youth he had been known as John Lackland. As compensation, he had married a great heiress, Hawisa of Gloucester. She was his cousin, so a dispensation from the Pope had to be obtained; it was, but not until after the astonishing decision that although married John and Hawisa must not bed together.

That was John's situation when in 1199, he who had owned so little, inherited (or took possession of) so much. Strictly speaking John's right to the throne was second to that of his elder brother's son, Arthur; but John took the throne and was generally accepted. In 1200 he was on the Continent, accepting homage from all the vassals who owed him allegiance. One of these was the Count of Angoulême, who had a very beautiful fourteen-year-old daughter, Isabella.

Even the coolest chroniclers record that John, who was thirty-four, became 'madly enamoured' of the beautiful girl.

She was already betrothed to a man called Hugh de Lusignan.

Betrothal was a contract, sometimes honoured, often broken. In defence of Isabella and her parents it must be said that John was their feudal overlord and he had the power, if it came to the point, of forbidding the marriage which should have followed the betrothal between Isabella and Lusignan for whom Isabella had some feeling as her later history showed.

John's marriage – really no marriage at all – was easily dissolved; Isabella wept and protested at the breaking of her betrothal, but she and her parents were helpless. She and the King of England were married in Bordeaux and then she came to England to be crowned.

We have some details of the expenses of that coronation; £12 was spent upon her clothing; but one chorister, for singing a special psalm was paid

£1. 5s., and the rushes spread on the floor cost rather more than that. The figures are comparatively disproportionate, but perhaps John's jealousy was already at work on two fronts; he did not wish her to outshine him, and he did not wish her to be too much admired, by other men.

He had been madly enamoured, certainly he was madly jealous and once when he suspected – without much reason – that she had taken a lover, he had the man hanged, and his corpse suspended over her bed.

Isabella bore a son who was to become Henry III, a daughter named Joanna and another named Isabella. Except when well-advanced in pregnancy she had gone with John wherever he went, and he was constantly on the move, for his was a troubled reign. One of his sworn enemies was, not unnaturally, the Hugh de Lusignan who had been robbed of his bride and was only pacified by a betrothal to Joanna, Isabella's daughter.

John had been a faithless son, a faithless brother and, on what evidence there is, a wicked uncle. It was generally believed at the time that he killed with his own hand, the boy, Arthur of Brittany, whose claim to the throne was better than his own. It could never be proved – murders are seldom committed before witnesses.

He was a notorious lecher and few people who drool over Magna Carta – that over-rated document which was only a re-hash of the one given by Henry I – ever consider that the barons' final attempt to bring John to heel was sparked off by his abduction and rape of a young noblewoman.

The kindest thing that can be said of John was that he was mad. In a rage he bit and gnawed things, or set fire to houses in which he had been entertained. He had a long-standing quarrel with the Pope who in the end excommunicated him – and all England with him, so that church doors were closed and their bells silent. With all England on the verge of revolt John settled his quarrel with the Pope on humiliating terms.

In October 1216 John was on his way to the North to deal with some still unruly barons. His journey took him across the Wash where an unexpectedly high tide swept away some of his baggage wagons, one of which carried the Crown Jewels which included the great crown of England. He arrived at Swineshead Abbey in Lincolnshire in a vicious bad temper, and at table that evening said that he hoped that he could make a half-penny loaf cost a shilling before the end of the year. What he was eating at the time is uncertain, some accounts mention peaches, others a dish of fine autumn pears. Perhaps he had both – monks were the best horticulturalists of the age.

Shortly afterwards he felt unwell, but he pushed on until he reached Newark, where he died. The question of poison arises inevitably – monks were skilled druggists, too; and that remark about the price of bread was tantamount to a declaration of war upon the people, especially the poor. There are two colourful stories about that evening at Swineshead; a Saxon

*Isabella lies with her parents-in-law and brother-in-law in the
Abbey at Fontevrault, where she took refuge in a 'secret chamber'.*

monk named Simon was so incensed by the remark that he went to his
Abbot and said that if he could be absolved beforehand he would give the
King a drink that would make all England glad. The Abbot agreed, but
when Simon presented the cup the King asked him to taste it first; and
Simon was dead in the Abbey infirmary before the King was dead at
Newark. The other story says that Simon presented the King with a fine
dish of pears, all but three of which he had pricked with a poisoned needle.
The King asked him to share the dish, which he did, taking the unpricked
ones.

In any case the King died and all England was glad. Isabella may have
shared the joy. She was in Gloucester when the news came and she had her
nine-year-old son Henry proclaimed there, crowned, for lack of a more
suitable coronet, with one of her golden collars.

She was not invited to have any part in the regency which was set up to rule until Henry became of age, so she left for her own home, Angoulême, and there was Hugh de Lusignan, still unmarried, for the little princess whose hand he had demanded as a peace-offering was still only a child. She was living in Hugh's castle, as her mother had once done during her betrothal.

Isabella was still young – about thirty – and still beautiful. After sixteen years of separation, Hugh and Isabella married.

The English were furious; they regarded Hugh de Lusignan as a follower of the King of France. They refused to pay Isabella the revenue to which, as Queen Mother, she was entitled – it included the income from those Cornish tin mines about which there had been trouble in Berengaria's day.

Henry III – he who had been crowned with his mother's necklet – was forced by his council to write to the Pope, asking him to excommunicate Hugh and Isabella for marrying without his consent. The Pope very sensibly decided that as Henry was under age his consent did not matter one way or the other and that the English were at fault in withholding Isabella's money.

The English then proposed a bargain; they would pay the revenue if they could have the young princess back. They were anxious to make peace with Scotland and the Scottish King fancied an English bride.

In France the war went on. Hugh de Lusignan changed his allegiance more than once. Isabella had more children, three sons, and several daughters before 1244, when two men, caught in an attempt to poison the King of France 'confessed' that Isabella had been the instigator of the plot. If this were true it showed a singular lack of sense on her part, for although under her influence Hugh had defected to the English side, Louis IX had forgiven him, restored the land he had lost and *apparently* taken him back into favour. Apparently, because Louis had a long memory, for when this scandal broke, he spoke of Hugh as being 'treason-spotted'.

Isabella made no attempt to stand and contest the charge. She fled to the Abbey of Fontevrault and there took refuge in a 'secret chamber'. Churches and religious houses could offer a certain degree of sanctuary to ordinary malefactors, but traitors were not supposed to be sheltered. However no attempt was made to bring her out to face trial, and she died, still in hiding, two years later and was buried, by her own request, in the open cemetery at Fontevrault. She was about sixty.

Her husband survived her by three years; once Isabella was dead he seems to have been cleared of his treason spots and actually died, covered with wounds, on Crusade, fighting side by side with the brother of the French King.

Years later, Isabella's son Henry III made a visit to Fontevrault and was shocked to see his mother lying in such a humble grave. He had her body moved, to lie inside the Abbey church, alongside Henry II, and Eleanor, and Richard I. Her effigy lies there still.

Eleanor of Provence

Queen to Henry III
born 1222, married 1236, died 1291

Eleanor of Provence was one of the most hated of the Queens of England, always regarded as a foreigner – though she was no more foreign than all but one – Henry I's Matilda – or most of those who came after her. Her mistake lay in her refusal to be assimilated and in her flagrant preference for foreigners – and this just at the time when the English were becoming aware of themselves as one people.

She was able to continue her misguided policy because she had so much influence over Henry III. It needed very little in the way of beauty or strength of character to gain ascendancy over Henry who was a remarkably weak-willed man; so weak of will that some people regarded him as half-witted.

Eleanor is said to have been beautiful and, in a literary way if in no other, she was clever – she was producing poetry in the romantic, Provençal style while she was still very young. It was in fact one of her poems which led to her becoming Queen of England. She wrote a poem about an ancient, half-mythical hero of Cornwall, and sent it, as a compliment, to Henry's younger brother, Richard of Cornwall, who appreciated such things. Henry appreciated them too. Knowing this and seeing his brother aged twenty-nine, with five abortive attempts to find a bride behind him, Richard commended Eleanor to Henry. And that was typical. Many men married women chosen for them, by parents, by political circumstance; few marry a wife selected by their younger brother.

Politically it was a good choice, in keeping with the deluded belief of the day – that blood kinship made for happy relationship in other spheres; Eleanor's elder sister was Queen of France.

*The woman portrayed in this early thirteenth-century French
head is not Eleanor of Provence but clearly shows a woman of
her qualities – beautiful and, in a literary way, clever.*

Eleanor landed at Dover accompanied by an impressive train of attendants. Wise kings in those days sent the bride's friends home, if not immediately, then as soon after the coronation as possible. Henry did not. He and
Eleanor were married at Canterbury in January 1236 and then she went to
London to be crowned.

It was a different coronation from that of her predecessor. Henry, like
his father, John, liked to be well-dressed himself, but he liked all about him
to be well-dressed, too. He spent lavishly. He was at once greedy to get and
ready to give. Eleanor's coronation was marked by vast expenditure, but
also by considerable gifts to the poor. She was young and pretty, and briefly
popular.

But the foreigners who had come with her stayed, and were joined by others. Any remunerative or honourable office that fell vacant was immediately bestowed upon a foreigner. At the dock known as Queenhythe, by tradition a perquisite of the Queen of England, foreign ships were given precedence over English ones. One can imagine the discontent amongst the merchants of London.

From the point of view of child-bearing, Eleanor was satisfactory; Edward, who was to be Edward I, was born at Westminster in 1239. He was named for the last undisputed King of England, Edward the Confessor; and that was a popular choice. But whatever popularity the birth of the heir and his name evoked, it was immediately cancelled out by Henry's hint that this was an occasion for valuable gifts. One noble said, 'Heaven gave us this child, but the King sells him to us'.

In Henry's defence – and therefore Eleanor's – it must be said that much of the money which was gathered by gifts or taxes, was well spent; Westminster Abbey was re-built, and Westminster Hall transformed from a stark, utilitarian building into a palace. And an orphanage was established and endowed. Eleanor bore another son, Edmund and several daughters; once the royal children were weighed, and their weight in silver given to the poor.

Eleanor lived through a civil war, short but savage, during which both her husband and her son Edward were taken prisoner by the rebel barons. Both were released unharmed and the worst thing that she suffered was to be pelted – when she attempted to leave the Tower of London where she was at the time – with clods of mud and filth from the streets. Irony here, for when she came to London for her coronation, Henry had ordered all London streets to be swept clean.

Henry died in 1272. His lasting faith in and devotion to his wife is proved by his will, made years earlier and never revoked. He appointed her Regent.

Regent she was never to be, for Edward, her eldest son was thirty-three, a hardened man of war. He had been on Crusade; he had learned, from one experience in the civil war, not to be too impetuous. And he never forgave what one might call the mob-element of London for throwing filth at his mother. She saw him crowned, and when she retired, as so many royal widows did, to a convent, he visited her as often as his busy, very busy, life permitted.

Not, on the whole, an unhappy story; she may not have endeared herself to the citizens of London or to those of high rank who had been supplanted by her foreign favourites, but her family relationships had been happy; a devoted husband, loving children and a fair length of days. She lived to hear of Edward's conquest of Wales. And she died at the end of the long, downward slide, called failing health.

Eleanora of Castile

First Queen to Edward I
born 1244, married 1254, died 1290

Eleanora, though she lived in troubled times, was a woman who had a happy life. It could have been otherwise, for hers was an arranged marriage, and took place when she was only ten. Edward, Prince of Wales was fifteen. Her brother, the King of Castile had insisted upon marriage, for English princes were rather apt to slide out of betrothals.

Astrologers had issued their verdict and predicted that all would be well if Edward and his mother reached Burgos, in Castile, on 5 August 1254; not a day earlier, not a day later. By careful timing of their journey Queen Eleanor and Prince Edward arrived at their destination at exactly the right date and the young couple were married.

The gap between the ages of bride and groom must have seemed wide at the moment. Edward, who when he reached full growth was to be six foot two inches tall, must even in his middle teens have been an impressive figure. He would be a man before she was out of childhood.

The little bride was well-received in England where Henry III had taken pains to see that she did not suffer too much from the English climate. Her chamber at Guildford Palace was to have glazed windows, a raised hearth and a chimney. She was also to have a wardrobe. These specifications are evidence of how rare such amenities were at the time.

While Eleanora was growing up and completing her education, Edward was busy with warfare, either mimic or real. He was said to haunt tournaments, and was at a very grand one in Paris when news reached him that the English barons had rebelled against his father. He hurried home and took part in the civil war which followed. Eleanora, for safety's sake, spent this period on the Continent.

When the war was over and Henry III firmly on his throne again, Eleanora was ready for real marriage, and for motherhood. She bore three

Eleanora of Castile, Edward I's chère reine, *stands proudly by his side on the front of Lincoln Cathedral.*

children in as many years. Henry III was so delighted with his grand-children that he gave their mother rich gifts of money and property.

Prince Edward was always restive when life was peaceful, so in 1269 he went on Crusade and Eleanora went with him. More was known now about the hardships and the dangers which a Crusade entailed and people warned Eleanora of what to expect. She said that nothing should part those whom God had joined and that the distance between Syria and Heaven was no greater than that between England and Heaven. She knew what she was about; Edward was a loving husband, but not a faithful one.

She was with him in Joppa when an assassin made an attempt upon his life. Contemporary stories speak of Edward having been struck by a

A fine gilt bronze effigy of Eleanora in Westminster Abbey.

poisoned dagger and of Eleanora sucking the poison from the wound. It is certain that Edward attributed his recovery – from the wound and the surgery which followed it – to the care and attention given him by his wife. Yet, when during his convalescence, he made his will, though he provided well for Eleanora, he left her no power, not even the custody of her children. This may not have been a slight, but a protective measure.

On this campaign, Eleanora bore her fourth child, a girl, called from her birthplace, Joanna of Acre.

The Crusade was a failure. Edward's reputation stood high – second only to that of Richard I – the assassination attempt proved that he was feared. But Edward realised that further struggle was futile and began to make his way home.

He and Eleanora were breaking their journey in Sicily when three messages reached them. Their elder son was dead. Their second son was dead. Henry III was dead.

The King of Sicily expressed his amazement that Edward had taken the deaths of his sons so calmly, and the death of his father so hard. Edward explained – a man could have more sons, but never another father.

And in fact children died very easily in those days; everything was against them. Centuries later, when hygiene and medicine had somewhat improved, a man said, 'All mine die,' as casually as he would have spoken of his cabbages. The very swaddling clothes which sound so nice in carols, meant that from its birth a child was wrapped like a mummy, stiff and immobile; the swaddling was supposed to keep the spine and the legs straight. And there were the many childhood diseases, for instance whooping cough, for which a fried mouse was reckoned to be a cure.

How Eleanora felt about the death of the two beautiful little boys whom she had left behind in order to follow Edward on Crusade is not recorded;

but she was again pregnant and perhaps agreed with Edward that a man –
and a woman – could have more sons. She had another, but he too slipped
away.

Eleanora's eighth child, and fourth son was born in the new, raw castle at
Caernarvon on the Welsh coast; for almost immediately after the extra-
ordinarily splendid coronation – bonfires on every hill, fountains of red
and white wine flowing, and five hundred splendid horses let loose, the
catcher to be the owner – Edward had turned to make war on Wales whose
ruler had refused to attend or to offer homage to him. The Welsh were
temporarily defeated, and Edward promised them a prince who could
speak no word of English – and produced his baby son. The baby who was
to become Edward II was recognised as Prince of Wales, a title worn proudly
by the eldest son of the King of England, from that day to this.

Edward was the idol of the City of London, and of the growing middle
class everywhere; he had never forgiven or forgotten how the barons had
treated his father and himself, or how the mob had behaved to his mother;
he liked the in-between people who under his strong and sensible rule, grew
prosperous. He expelled all Jews whose businesses thus fell into other hands.

He had dreams of a United Kingdom, and with Wales apparently quiet,
the strong border castles held by strong men, he turned his attention to
Scotland. With thirteen contenders for the throne there, the time seemed
ripe for intervention. In 1290 he left rather hurriedly for Scotland. Eleanora
was 'to pack and follow'.

She had a good deal of household equipment – the list reads like an inven-
tory of Aladdin's cave; cups and plates, knives, jugs, drinking vessels all of
gold, or silver or silver-gilt. It is commonly believed that forks were unknown in England at the time, but Eleanora had two, one of silver, one of
crystal. Still, with so much to be packed, Eleanora was not far behind;
Edward had not reached the Scottish border when she reached Grantham
in Lincolnshire, and there fell ill. Lincolnshire was then mainly fenland, and
all fenlands bred fevers.

When Edward heard that Eleanora was ill, he turned straight back and
rode hard, but she was dead when he arrived.

She must be buried at Westminster; and for thirteen days the funeral
procession moved southwards; at every place where her body stayed for a
night, Edward ordered a memorial cross to be erected, to his *chère reine*. As
the cortège neared London all the principal citizens, clad in black, lined the
roads and when she was interred Edward arranged for Masses and dirges
and for two wax tapers to burn for ever by her tomb. They burned until
the Reformation, three hundred years later. And one by one all but three
of the crosses vanished. But how many of the hurrying thousands who use
Charing Cross station every day associate its name with Eleanora, Edward's
chère reine?

Marguerite of France, though perhaps not as beautiful as her elder sister, was nevertheless obviously a striking woman as this sculpture from Lincoln Cathedral shows.

Marguerite of France

Second Queen to Edward I
born 1282, married 1298, died 1318

A brisk second marriage is not necessarily a denigration of the dead; it is on the whole the people who have been unhappily married who say, 'Never again'; Edward I was getting on in years, but he had always liked women. During his knight-errant days, waiting for Eleanora to grow up, he had given many men cause for jealousy, and there are indications that he had not always been strictly as faithful in body as in mind to his *chère reine*. He was a Plantagenet and that meant vigour, in whatever direction it was applied. Edward I had loved one Queen and was prepared to love another. Within a year of Eleanora's burial he was negotiating for another bride, the sister of the King of France.

Matrimonially, Edward was far less desirable than he had been at the time of his first marriage. He had his heir, Edward of Caernarvon, so no girl who married him was likely to become Queen Mother; and he was getting old, no girl who married him could count on being Queen of England for long.

Philip of France considered these things and decided not to waste his elder sister, a very beautiful girl, on the ageing King of England; so although her name, Blanche, appears in the preliminary negotiations – Edward was to pay for the alliance by surrendering Gascony to the French – it was her younger sister, Marguerite who actually became Edward's second wife. She was sixteen.

Hers is rather a bleak story. Edward, who had turned away from a most promising situation in Scotland in order to reach his first Queen's sick-bed, had not even time to spare to give his second wife a proper coronation; yet she was acknowledged as his Queen, and followed his campaigns much as Eleanora had done. When she stayed behind she resided chiefly in the Tower of London and Edward ordered that no-one should approach her with a petition for fear that some contagious disease should afflict her. When he

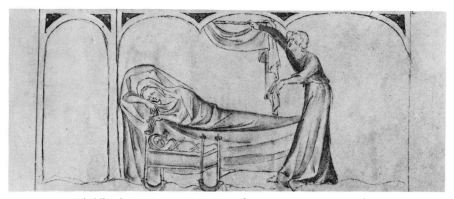

Childbirth in Marguerite's time; from a contemporary psalter.

was victorious in Scotland he sent for her to share his triumph. And, old as he was, be begot two sons, Thomas and Edmund.

Edward of Caernarvon frequently provoked his father who did not hold that even princes should break the law with impunity and twice sentenced him to spells of a mild form of imprisonment. But he always forgave him, partly because he was the son of his *chère reine*, partly because he was a good soldier. They were together, still fighting the troublesome Scots in 1307 when Edward I, aged sixty-eight, died. His final charge to his son was typical of a man whose life had been a mixture of warfare and happy domesticity. Edward II was to continue with the war against the Scots; and he was to take good care of his step-mother and two young step-brothers.

Marguerite was only twenty-six, and might reasonably have been expected to mourn for a while and then re-marry; but she said, 'When Edward died, all men died to me'.

She did not spend as much time in mourning seclusion as was usual for royal widows for she knew that Edward I had set his heart on his son's marriage to Isabella of France. So she accompanied him to Boulogne and saw him married to her niece, who presently was to be known as the She-Wolf of France. With that safely accomplished Marguerite retired from public life and spent the ten years that remained to her in good works – not merely gifts to the poor but encouraging historians and architects. Amongst the buildings for which she was largely responsible was the Grey Friars' church, in London.

Edward II gave every evidence of being fond of his step-mother, and while she lived Marguerite is said to have exercised influence for the good on Isabella. Not perhaps too difficult, for Isabella was only thirteen at the time of her marriage, and only twenty-three when her aunt died.

Through the marriages of her sons, and her grandchildren – one granddaughter married Edward, the Black Prince – Marguerite was to be claimed as ancestress by many noble families, and by future Queens.

Isabella of France

Queen to Edward II
born 1292, married 1308, died 1358
See colour plate facing page 65.

What is it, inside us all which makes a more ready response to vice than to virtue? Walk down any street and somebody says, 'There goes a good woman'. Who takes a second look? Somebody says, 'There goes a bad woman', and interest quickens. *Why* bad? *How* bad?

Like every other princess, Isabella of France is described as 'Fair'. The word deserves a moment's consideration. When we say fair we mean blonde and to an extent our forbears meant the same. Most princesses were blonde, for the purely Nordic people who, under various names, had over-run all Western Europe had fair or fair-to-red hair and eyes of varying shades of blue-grey-green. Even in Spain, which one associates with dark colouring, the royal family and many of the noble families were fair-to-reddish.

But for our ancestors 'fair', especially when applied to a girl, meant a complexion unblemished by small-pox. And that was comparatively rare. Almost everybody had small-pox and most were marked. But for those who could afford what was called 'the red treatment', or 'the red system', there was hope of emerging unscathed. Edward II had himself suffered from small-pox and his physician said, 'I ordered the Prince to be enveloped in scarlet cloth and that his bed, and all the furniture thereof, should be of a bright red colour; which practice not only cured him but prevented his being marked'.

Just another old wives' tale? Just another superstition? Far from it. In this century it has been discovered that some ray in light encourages scarring, and can be excluded by a red screen.

So a princess – or any girl fortunate enough to be born with light hair and eyes, and to have emerged from the small-pox unpocked – was fair.

Isabella of France was fair. She was called Isabella the Fair, until the more interesting name of She-Wolf of France was bestowed upon her.

She was fair, and she had the highest pedigree of any English Queen before her. So what went wrong? Is what I would like to find

Edward and Isabella landed at Dover and were joined there by a man of comparatively lowly birth – Piers Gaveston. He had been born in Guienne, so was reckoned as a foreigner by the English; yet it was to him, and not to any nobleman, that Edward had entrusted England during his absence.

Perhaps it was not unusual in those uninhibited days for men, meeting after a brief parting, to fall upon each others' necks and kiss. Two days later Isabella noticed something more sinister. Her father, at the wedding, had given Edward II some exceptionally valuable presents, gold rings and chains and jewels. Now Gaveston was wearing them.

Then came the coronation, and the man chosen for the highest honour of all – that of offering the crown – was Gaveston, who on this occasion was even more magnificently clad than the King himself.

Isabella was young, but, contrary to modern theories, people matured earlier then. She understood, and in her first letter to her father she described herself as the most wretched wife in the world. There was nothing that he could do about it except to determine that when the chance came he would do his best to injure his son-in-law.

Despite this first complaining letter, Isabella set to work to make the best of things. When Edward quarrelled with any baron, or group of barons, she acted as mediator, often with success. When Edward resumed the war with Scotland, she went with him and was once almost captured when the Scots made an out-flanking move. In every way her behaviour was impeccable and she enjoyed great popularity. This was increased when in 1312 she gave birth at Windsor to her first child, the boy who was to become Edward III. No doubt was ever cast on his paternity. The Queen had an unsullied reputation then, and a tendency towards homosexuality did not prevent a man from fathering children. Two years later she bore a second son, and then, after another two years, a daughter.

Edward became steadily more unpopular; he had once shown promise as a soldier; but he proved to be no leader; vacillating, procrastinating, ineffectual.

Even his behaviour towards his favourite was extraordinary. At one point he banished him to his native Guienne – but sent him off laden with every portable valuable he could lay hands on. Then he recalled him, protected him against the jealous rage of the barons, and finally abandoned him. Gaveston was given a sham trial and hanged. One of the charges brought against him was that he had attained his power over the King by means of witchcraft – Gaveston's mother had been burned as a witch.

Edward lost no time in replacing him, taking this time two favourites, father and son, the Despensers. Such a triangular relationship in such circumstances, tends to show that though Edward might be fond, the Despensers were not; they were aiming at power and wealth.

It is difficult to pinpoint the moment when Isabella took a lover. It is indeed difficult to understand how any one of the many Queens who have been accused of adultery ever managed the mechanics of the business. Privacy was the rarest of luxuries for everybody until comparatively recent times, and Queens have never enjoyed it, ladies-in-waiting, waiting women, pages, sentries in every passage, at every turn of the stairs.

There was civil war – and famine – in England again. Isabella was safely and comfortably installed in the Tower of London, awaiting the birth of another child, when two men, Roger Mortimer, Lord of Chirk and Roger Mortimer, his nephew, fell into the hands of the pro-Edward barons and were sent to the Tower, sentenced to death. Theirs was no token imprisonment; it was rigorous, and the older man soon died. Some influence behind the scenes contrived to have the death sentence upon young Roger Mortimer postponed; and then his escape organised. His guards were drugged, good horses awaited him on the other side of the river and he went to Paris, where Isabella's brother had just succeeded as King. There, no doubt, he was eloquent about what Isabella had been obliged to put up with. Isabella's father had given covert support to his son-in-law's enemies, rebel barons or Scots; her brother went further and said he would confiscate some of the land which Edward held from him as a liege.

Then the utter weakness of Edward's character was most fully exposed. Isabella offered to go and mediate between her husband and her brother, and Edward let her go.

Once safe in France, Isabella sent messages to Edward. All could be amicably arranged if he sent their son – now a youth of fifteen – to France, to do allegiance to the new King and take possession of the disputed territory. Edward sent him.

Isabella then announced that neither she nor the heir would return to England until the Despensers were banished.

She had her reasons. Gaveston may have stolen her husband's affection for her, but the Despensers had been her active enemies; they had persuaded the King to cut down her revenues, so that Edward, who at first had been generous to her, had become as far as she was concerned a miser. She had even been deprived of those tin mines in Cornwall.

Edward, instead of agreeing – or pretending to agree – to this rational condition, wrote letters. Letters to Isabella, letters to the King of France, letters to young Edward; remarkable letters, eloquent, pitiable, obstinate, and false. In them he refers to the Despensers as his good friends and supporters – and refers to Isabella's evil behaviour with Roger Mortimer. Of all these outpourings that was the one to make its mark; the King of France decided not to support his sister.

Isabella set about recruiting men to her cause and when in September

1326 she landed in England – where, authorities differ; one says Harwich, one says Orwell – she had with her almost three thousand men, their nationalities and their motives as mixed as those of the men who had come with William the Conqueror in 1066. She had her son, her lover and Lord John of Hainault; and she knew that she could count upon the support of a great number of the English nobility; and, given a modicum of luck, that of many ordinary people who were tired of Edward's misrule.

Edward behaved in his usual fatuous way. He wrote more letters, to the King of France; to the Pope. He issued a proclamation offering a thousand pounds for the head of Roger Mortimer. Isabella smartly replied with an offer of two thousand pounds for the younger Despenser – his father was hardly worth bothering about.

Then Edward, seeing how men flocked towards Isabella and her son, tried to escape, to the West, to Lundy. (We are told that we must not speak of the Isle of Lundy because Lundy itself means island.) He never reached that bleak sanctuary. The Queen's forces overtook him and he was sent to Kenilworth Castle to wait while his enemies deliberated.

About the fate of the Despensers nobody deliberated; the father was hanged in the ordinary way; the son, more spectacularly, crowned with nettles on a gibbet fifty feet high.

Edward II was formally deposed and Edward III acknowledged.

Whether Edward II's terrible fate should be mentioned here is debatable. He was shuffled about from castle to castle and ended in Berkeley where he was murdered. Mysteriously. Almost certainly by the Queen's order. How? It is said that some terrible screams were heard and that no outward injury was to be seen on his body. A fairly general consensus agrees upon a red-hot iron being thrust into his anus. Given the ruthless behaviour of the times – and what homosexuality means – it could be likely.

Isabella, no mean tactician, set about lightening the gloom by arranging Edward III's marriage to Philippa of Hainault. Not, by the standards of the time, a very grand match, but when thrown out of the French Court she had found friends in the petty province, and of the Count of Hainault's four pretty daughters, Edward had seemed to prefer the youngest. (Theirs was to be, for a while at least, another fairy-tale story.)

Isabella's popularity was however waning. She had been acclaimed as 'The Liberator'; but why do away with the Despensers just to make way for Roger Mortimer?

Isabella and the barons of England were now dealing with a very different man from Edward II. Edward III was Edward II's son, but he was Edward I's grandson, much like him in appearance and character.

Edward took action against Roger Mortimer, had him arrested and hanged – the first person to be executed at Tyburn. Then he issued a proclamation designed to clear his mother's name; Mortimer, he said, was to

Isabella returning from France, in conversation with Sir John Hainault, from a fourteenth-century manuscript.

blame for everything, he had by lies brought about the estrangement between Isabella and her husband; he had robbed the royal treasury. But while trying thus publicly to clear his mother's name, Edward did not behave as though he believed in her innocence. He confiscated all her wealth and limited her to an income of a thousand pounds a year – a comfortable sum at the time but not large enough for the upkeep of a royal household.

In fact her son did not intend Isabella to live in great style; nor did he intend to allow her to be at liberty to meddle in affairs and stir up more trouble. He ordered her to live at Castle Rising, in Norfolk, one of those stern Norman fortresses with walls three feet thick. She was not allowed to go out, and it needed a permit from the King to visit her.

Yet Edward kept up appearances by visiting her himself two or three times a year – once with his Queen; and so long as he lived no-one was allowed to say or write a word in any way derogatory to her. Isabella sat out thirty-one years in this backwater, with just one visit to London when some financial tangle needed her presence at its resolving.

Some chroniclers believe that during this long time she was inter-mittently deranged. Her first fit of madness is said to have occurred when Roger Mortimer was hanged.

It is likely. Her marriage had never been more than a half-and-half affair; and she was a woman who was inclined to throw herself whole-heartedly into any situation. She had been whole-hearted in keeping up the pretence that all was well between her and Edward II, until pretence was no longer possible. She had then been whole-hearted in waging war upon him. She was probably just as whole-hearted about her love affair – a proper man who loved her. He was condemned not only to be hanged at Tyburn but to dangle there, in chains for three days. Enough to make the woman who had loved him have what is described as a violent access of madness. And then all those dull years with nothing to plan for, nothing to hope for.

It has long been the rule, though not until this century openly expressed, that a woman can get away with anything, even murder, so long as her sexual sheet is clean. It was adultery, not murder that took Edith Thompson to the gallows and it is certain that had Isabella not taken a lover, her story would have been very different. Instead of being the shamed, imprisoned creature that she was, she would have retained her title of 'The Liberator', the one who had saved England from a weak and disastrous rule and put a strong king on the throne. She would have been, not one of the most dishonoured Queens, but one of the most honoured.

It is possible that she was demented and because demented, lived to be sixty-three; most demented people reach a tolerable age.

When she died, her son, keeping up appearances, had her body brought to London, to lie in the Grey Friars' church. And he ordered that London's filthy streets should be cleaned in honour of the occasion. What remained of Roger Mortimer, after three days in chains at Tyburn, had been laid within Grey Friars', so she lay beside him, at last.

But her story does not end there.

That old, schizophrenic idea that though a woman could not inherit a throne and rule, her male issue could claim inheritance through her, was at work again. Isabella's brother had died leaving no direct heir, and Edward III claimed, through his mother, the throne of France.

So what is somewhat casually called the Hundred Years War began.

Philippa
of Hainault

Queen to Edward III
born 1314, married 1328, died 1369

Philippa was young when she came to England to marry Edward III, not yet in full control; her wedding was magnificent, but her coronation, in 1330, was not conspicuously glorious. Three months later, she was a mother; her first child, Edward, later renowned as the Black Prince, was born at Woodstock in 1330. A good strong boy; and breast fed by his mother. Nowadays such a fact would not be worth mentioning, but in 1330 and in recurrent cycles of fashion it was unusual for women of rank and wealth not to hire a wet nurse. Something of sense and something of superstition went into the choice of a wet nurse; it was sensible to engage a young, healthy woman, immune to small-pox because she had lived through it; it was superstition to believe that something of the woman's character could be imbibed with her milk.

It was while young Edward's birth was being celebrated that Philippa showed her influence over her fierce-tempered husband. There was to be a great tournament, held, not on a tourney-ground but in a public street in Cheapside, the highway thickly sanded to prevent the horses from slipping. A temporary gallery was erected to accommodate the Queen and ladies of the nobility, and they were no sooner in their places than the whole thing collapsed. Nobody suffered actual injury but all the ladies were shaken and shocked. Edward swore that the carpenters who had built so carelessly should die – a fairly normal reaction in any fond husband – but Philippa, still trembling and in disarray, pleaded on her knees that they should be forgiven, and the King relented. It reads almost like a rehearsal for the famous story of the Burghers of Calais.

Edward showed his faith in Philippa by appointing her as Regent when he went to the Continent to fight for the French throne to which he made claim through his mother. This was the beginning of the long, destructive

A contemporary travelling coach; Queen Philippa may be one of the ladies portrayed in this illumination from the Luttrell Psalter.

struggle which was to grumble on for roughly a hundred years. It had brief moments of glory, Crécy and Agincourt. Crécy was not merely a great victory for the English – it was the warning bell, heralding the end of the feudal age; for it was proved on that August day in 1346 that the ordinary man, armed with the formidable long-bow, was more than a match for a mounted knight in full armour. Pulled by a strong arm, the iron-tipped arrow of the long-bow could pierce a plank of oak six inches thick.

In that same year, with Edward III overseas, the Scots seized the opportunity to invade the north of England and penetrated almost as far as Durham. Philippa, with a hastily raised, somewhat makeshift army, met them at Neville's Cross and drove them back. The King of Scotland was taken prisoner and spent so long in the Tower that one suspects Philippa of not putting forward any vehement plea for mercy on his behalf.

As well as defending her adopted country, this Queen enriched it. She came from Flanders, always the best customer for English wool, which was woven and dyed by Flemings and then sold back to England as cloth. Philippa persuaded some of her fellow-countrymen to come to England to ply their skills. A colony of them settled in Norwich, and as their patron she often visited them. When possible her visits were timed to coincide with Edward's visits to his mother at Castle Rising.

In 1348 there came to England the terrible plague known as the Black Death. It had been creeping westwards out of Asia for years and reached

*A feast of the kind at which Philippa would have enjoyed
herself; from the Luttrell Psalter.*

England in the autumn, generally regarded as a fairly healthy time in
England, since the autumn rains cleared the filthy streets and the foul water-
ways, and the chillier weather put an end to the variety of what were called
summer fevers. It is known now that the black rat carried the plague, and
rats abounded on the ships which took fighting men to France and brought
home the wounded, and the corpses of those whose families could afford to
bring bodies home and have them buried in English soil. There was plenty
of merchant shipping too, exports of wool, imports of wine. Once on an
island where nobody had either an acquired or an inborn immunity, the
Black Death ran riot, and in a few months halved the population, and as
Crécy had shown the value of the ordinary man in a military sense, so the
Black Death showed his value as a cog in the economic machine. Serfs, for
generations tied to the land they tilled and the overlord who owned it,
broke away, demanded wages.

There was one person, at least, to whom the Black Death was merciful;
this was Philippa's daughter, Joanna who was actually on her way to marry
a Castilian Prince who even in that merciless age was to be known as Pedro
the Cruel, when she was struck down by the plague and died.

It is perhaps a little sad to think that Edward III did not remain faithful to
Philippa who had served him so well in so many ways. But age dimmed her
beauty, and he was a Plantagenet, one of a family of prodigious energy and
rapacious appetite in all spheres. Like many other Queens, Philippa ignored

these little lapses and when she died, at Windsor, one of her favourite residences, Edward III was holding her hand.

She had borne and reared many children – perhaps too many for England's good, for it was between the descendants of her sons, Edward, the Black Prince and John of Gaunt that civil war was to arise.

She died in 1369 and was buried in Westminster Abbey.

Edward outlived her by eight years; and when he died nobody held his hand. He had fallen into the clutches of a harpy named Alice Perrers and when he ceased to breathe, in his palace of Sheen near Richmond, she stripped the rings from his fingers and made off with them.

About Philippa, during her life-time there had been no breath of scandal; in fact a chronicler recording her death spoke of her as the most courteous, liberal and noble lady. As such she had lived, as such she was buried.

But a few years later an extraordinary story went about.

It ran thus; her son, John of Ghent, or Gaunt as the English called him, was not the son of Edward III. Philippa had borne a daughter and rather than disappoint Edward III had had smuggled in a boy, son of a labouring man of Ghent; and she had brought him up as John of Gaunt.

Whoever invented this story, supposed to have been confided on her death-bed to William of Wykeham, founder of Winchester College, did not take family resemblances into account. John of Gaunt was as typical a Plantagenet as any of them. But the nasty little story hung about and soured John of Gaunt's temper and made him a difficult subject.

*Philippa, from a copy of her effigy
in Westminster Abbey.*

*A detail from Berengaria of Navarre's tomb in the Abbey
of L'Epau, near Le Mans.*

Anne of Bohemia

First Queen to Richard of Bordeaux, Richard II
born 1366, married 1382, died 1394

The first-born son of Edward III and Philippa of Hainault, Edward, the Black Prince, did not live to inherit the throne, but he left an heir, a boy who was eleven when his grandfather died. This boy, Richard II, was still being controlled by the Council of Regency, when at the age of sixteen he married Anne, a daughter of the Emperor Charles IV – a princess from a far country.

A few people in London knew that there was in central Europe a country called Bohemia, with a capital called Prague; a few people in Prague knew that far to the West there was an island with London as its capital; but the contact between the two countries was so slight that when the match between Richard and Anne was first proposed, Anne's mother, before giving her consent, had England inspected. Was it a fit place for her daughter to live in? Apparently the report was favourable, for the young Princess was allowed to set out to become Queen of England. She was fifteen, very beautiful, well-educated.

It is pleasant to think that she and Richard were happy together, for the times were far from happy; England was being torn by every imaginable strife, social, religious and political. One trouble was that the King had uncles – John of Gaunt was one – all stern, war-like men, who thought that they could govern better than a boy whose tastes were literary and musical rather than martial.

In the eye of the hurricane there is always an eye of calm, and it was in this tenuous security that Richard and Anne lived for sixteen years.

Isabella of France in armour, with her troops at Hereford.
The body of Hugh Despenser is seen in the background,
from a fourteenth-century manuscript illustration.

A copy of the effigy of Anne of Bohemia which lies beside that of her husband Richard II in Westminster Abbey.

Anne seldom intervened in public affairs, but she did protect Wycliffe who might justly be called the Father of the Reformation. She owned a bible and read it; and although Wycliffe's followers, known as Lollards, were severely put down in England, it was indirectly through Anne that Wycliffe's 'Protestantism' got its first toehold on the Continent. After her death her Bohemian attendants and servants went back to Bohemia, taking Lollardry with them.

Anne also made a contribution to fashion which sounds too trivial to be worthy of mention, but for which many dead women and many dead horses would decry her. She introduced the side-saddle. Not quite as we know it from pictures, but ill-balanced enough. Until her time English women who rode on horseback, rode astride, the weight evenly balanced; after Anne's innovation, both the female rider's legs on one side, a lot of horses had sore backs and all ladies rode in a cramped and precarious posture.

Even about this there is a touch of irony; riding astride in the old fashion had often been blamed for miscarriages. Anne of Bohemia, riding a clumsy

*This nineteenth-century painting by J. R. Herbert recreates a
fourteenth-century scene of a noblewoman, mounted side-saddle,
arriving at St Augustine's Monastery, Canterbury.*

side-saddle, never, so far as we know, became pregnant at all.

She died, very suddenly, struck down by the plague, possibly not in any
way connected with the great epidemic, just a summer plague, in June
1394, at her favourite palace at Richmond.

Richard was quite literally inconsolable. In a rough and turbulent world
she had been his true partner, sharer of his taste for the more beautiful things
in life.

Since Anne had died childless there was considerable pressure brought
to bear upon Richard to marry again, beget a child.

Many Plantagenets had in their make-up a slippery element and Richard II
had his share of it. He dodged all the proposed alliances and chose to marry
a child of eight years old, Isabella, daughter of the King of France, against
whom all the militant men in England were eager to resume war. They
protested, they said she was too young and Richard answered, we are told
'pleasantly', that every day would make her older. Richard was now of full
age, apparently in full control, and like many people overmuch suppressed
in youth, inclined to be defiant. So he had his way.

Isabella
of Valois

Second Queen to Richard II, known as the Little Queen
born 1387, married 1395, died 1410

She was little when she came to England in 1395; between eight and nine years old. Richard's perverse choice of a second wife inspired so much curiosity that nine people were crushed to death in the crowd anxious to look at her.

She was crowned, with great splendour and then sent to Windsor to grow up. Richard visited her, bringing gifts, making jokes, behaving towards her as an elder brother. And then going away.

How did she feel when he went away forever?

It happened in 1399 when she was still very young. The long, grumbling civil war between York and Lancaster halted with the triumph of the Lancastrian, Henry of Bolingbroke who deposed Richard and had himself crowned; Henry IV.

Isabella was still a child, between the age of twelve and thirteen, when she was obliged to move from Windsor, because the new King wanted to take possession of his royal residence. She, her attendants and her belongings were moved to Sunninghill, and there she sat and waited and heard many tales; some true, some false.

It was true that Richard had been taken prisoner and placed under strict guard at Pontefract Castle. It was *not* true that he had escaped. That was a tale put about by the Yorkists who would not accept Henry IV's rule. To back it up they had a man, somewhat resembling Richard in appearance and dressed in clothes similar to his. They did not bring this man into Isabella's presence, for she would have discovered the imposture at once. But they told her that Richard was on his way south, at the head of an army of a hundred thousand men; and that what she must do was to put herself at the head of the local rebels and go to meet him.

London in the late fourteenth century. The poet, Charles of
Orleans, Isabella's second husband, is seen at the window in the Tower.

This she did, and got as far as Cirencester. The mayor there was a Lancastrian, and he betrayed them. The two leading rebels, the Earls of Kent and Salisbury, were executed without trial. Isabella was too young to be held responsible; also she was the daughter of the King of France; and Henry IV was already making plans for her. He planned a marriage between her and his heir.

This young man, Shakespeare's Prince Hal, one day to be the hero of Agincourt was then eleven years old, handsome and likeable, but Isabella refused to have anything to do with him. She regarded Henry IV as a usurper. Richard's fate was shrouded in mystery, and the details of his murder were never known, but the fact that another marriage was being proposed for her proved that Richard must be dead. She went into deep mourning.

Henry mistakenly believed that by shutting her away, with only a few ladies to attend her, would make her change her mind. It did not.

*This panel of the Virgin and Child is a fine example of the high
quality that stained glass attained during the reign of Richard II.
It was commissioned by William of Wykeham for Winchester
College and was executed by Thomas Glazier of Oxford in 1393,
just before Isabella of Valois came to England.*

The French then demanded her back, and Henry played for time, assuring
them that she was safe and well-cared for, enjoying her dower rights and
being treated as befitting her rank.

As Richard had said, she was growing older every day; but she still wore
black, still refused to have anything to do with the usurper or his family, and
at last even Henry, a tenacious man, gave way and returned her to her own
country. She arrived back in France wearing her widow's clothing.

That her objection had been to having anything to do with the Lancastrian
family and not to the idea of re-marriage was shown when she did re-marry,
choosing her cousin, the Duke of Orleans, a poet and the most accomplished
man in Europe. They had a very happy, but brief marriage; Isabella died
bearing her first child. She was just twenty-two.

Her husband lived on to fight her one-time suitor at Agincourt, where
he was taken prisoner. Because of his nearness to the French throne he was
denied the customary ransom and spent twenty-five years in the Tower of
London, where he produced some of his best poetry.

Joanna of Navarre

Queen to Henry IV
born about 1370, married 1403, died 1437

Joanna's is one of the names which the average person, asked to make a list of our Queens, would almost certainly omit; yet her seventy years of life were crammed with drama and intrigue enough to make several novels.

She was born in or around the year 1370, the second daughter of a King of Navarre known as Charles the Bad. Such a nickname was not easily come by in the fourteenth century, but even then there were things which decent men would not do. Charles the Bad would do anything if it furthered his ambition to obtain the throne of France, to which he considered he had a claim through his mother. The story of his efforts is riddled with incidents of broken faith, a complete disregard for any code of chivalry and downright crime. He was inclined to poison people who stood in his way.

When Joanna was eleven, she and her two brothers were taken prisoner by the French and held as hostages for their father's good behaviour. Since he was incapable of good behaviour their lives could have been in danger, but the French were chivalrous, and their time in Paris was spent in comfort. It may have been during that time that she acquired her elegance and her sense of style.

The children were finally freed through the intervention of the King of Castile.

In 1386 Joanna was married to the Duke of Brittany – a typical political marriage. Her father promised her a grand dowry – naturally never paid. Despite this, and despite the fact that her husband had been married twice before and was in declining health, the marriage was reasonably happy; she produced the heir to the Duchy and was, it is recorded, a kind and attentive wife to an ailing, ageing man.

Her second marriage, which made her Queen of England, was also politically motivated. Henry of Bolingbroke, a descendant of the Lancastrian line, had made himself King of England, but he needed all the support he could get on the Continent. Marrying the mother of the young Duke of Brittany would obtain him an ally; and doubtless Joanna thought that by marrying the King of England she would make an alliance which would protect her son and his inheritance.

When she became Queen of England she was thirty-three; Henry was thirty-seven, and he also had been married before; he already had his heir.

This was another marriage of convenience which turned out well – to Joanna's credit. She and Henry were married at Winchester in February 1403 and three weeks later she was crowned at Westminster, having been given a good reception by the people.

Her appearance, we read, was majestic, an impression surely increased by a head-dress, two feet high, made of gauze stretched over a wire frame.

Joanna's popularity was short-lived. The principal charge against her at this time seems to be that she was avaricious, not an uncommon fault, and one to which people who have suffered insecure childhoods are very prone. She seems to have exercised her influence over Henry in the interests of mercy. To his children she was a good step-mother.

Henry IV was not an easy man to deal with; he was irascible, jealous and of a morbid turn of mind. He had expended so much energy on obtaining the throne that at forty he was prematurely aged. As a young man he had been handsome, but towards the end of his life he contracted leprosy and became so disfigured that he could not appear in public. He was inclined to think that the disease was a punishment for his sins. He died when he was forty-seven.

Joanna was not Queen Mother, but for a time she was treated as such. Henry V gave her permission to reside in any of his royal castles and added to her already considerable wealth by further gifts.

Why was she arrested in 1419 on the charge of being a witch and seeking by sorcery to do harm to Henry who was then in Normandy? Why was her step-son, who had always referred to her as his 'dear Mother', so easily turned against her? And who thought he was serving any purpose by poisoning the King's mind? We are given few details; there is no record of the trial – if indeed she had one. She was in her own palace at Havering Bower when by order of the Duke of Bedford who was acting as Regent, she was arrested, and taken to Leeds and kept in close confinement. Henry sent word that she should be stripped of all her possessions, even her spare clothes were taken.

The actual accusation was first made by her confessor, a Minorite friar; and perhaps the mystery of it all will never be unravelled because shortly after her arrest he had a quarrel with another cleric who strangled him.

It was an age very much concerned with heresy, and to many people heresy and witchcraft were practically synonymous; and it is true that

'Uneasy lies the head that wears a crown'. Joanna of Navarre lying beside her husband, Henry IV who looks older than his forty-seven years, in Canterbury Cathedral.

Navarre was a Basque country, practising a very polluted form of Christianity, with some customs, such as crowning their King under a certain tree, that are said to have been derived from the Assyrians. But Joanna had lived in England for sixteen years and anything unorthodox about her religion would surely have revealed itself earlier. Why should she – even if she had the power – wish to harm Henry V who had been so generous to her?

We do know that a few months before her sudden arrest Henry had been trying to borrow from her – the war with France proving expensive; we do know that he took possession of all that she owned.

Joanna was moved from Leeds to Pevensey, but still kept in close and wretched confinement. It had lasted almost four years when the hero of Agincourt, the darling of the English, with the complete conquest of northern France within sight, fell ill of dysentery, that scourge of armies. He lay ill for a month, and somewhere during that time began to suspect that he might not recover and amongst the things which he said troubled his conscience was his treatment of his step-mother. He sent word to his Council that she was to be released, set free to live wherever she wished and that all her property should be restored to her. She was to be provided with cloth for gowns, 'such as she useth to wear'.

It could have been his troubled conscience – even very tough characters had tender consciences in those days. It could have been something else – a belief in magic; for here he was, only thirty-three years old, a seasoned soldier, strongest of the strong, bravest of the brave, brought low by the most humiliating of all ailments. It is possible that in 1419 Henry had chosen to believe the unsubstantiated charges brought against Joanna and used them as an excuse to seize her property and enrich himself; it is possible that in his last days he hoped that full restitution would placate her.

He died.

Joanna lived on, very comfortably, though some of her confiscated property could not be recovered, some had been sold, or mortgaged; still, enough was salvaged to enable her to live 'in all princely prosperity'. Nobody, so far as we are told, ever mentioned the matter of witchcraft again. Henry VI, her step-grandson, showed her every respect as soon as he was old enough to do so.

She died and was buried at Canterbury, beside her husband, Henry IV and quite near the shrine of Thomas-à-Becket. She is the only Queen of England ever to have been *punished* for witchcraft – many years later there were mutterings about Anne Boleyn – and she must be one of the very few women who escaped unscathed from the charge, so easy to bring, so difficult to refute. Her ghost was for a long time believed to walk in her favourite dwelling at Havering Bower. Again one asks, *why?*

Catherine of Valois

Queen to Henry V
born 1401, married 1420, died 1437

Sometimes history throws up something too evanescent to be called a clue; just a breath, a whisper, a speculation. This is one.

Shakespeare wrote a play about Henry V; in it is one of the most stirring exhortations of all time.

Shakespeare also wrote a play about the Taming of the Shrew.

Was it by accident that the Shrew's name should be Katharine?

Catherine was the much younger sister of Isabella whom Henry, as Prince of Wales, had wooed unavailingly; she was a French princess – and France lay wounded and helpless at Henry's feet. The marriage was part of the peace treaty.

Did Henry V expect a meek and amenable spouse?

She had a splendid coronation on 24 February 1421, though, as some official explained, since it was now Lent, only fish could be served, but what fish! Conger eel, bream, sole, chub, roach, smelt and lobster, all with the appropriate accompaniments, called subtleties. Present at this meal was the King of Scots who had been a prisoner, kindly treated, but a prisoner, for many years. At this, her wedding feast, Catherine begged Henry to release him. Henry did so.

Presently the Queen was pregnant. Henry V, for all his glorious victories in France, was still having trouble in England where a number of people favoured another branch of the family. So he often went on progress, showing himself to the people who were rather susceptible to exhibitions of power, and to feasts, and to gifts. He went on one of these progresses, to the always-unsettled North. Then he was called away to deal with a situation which had flared up in France. So he could not watch over his wife in the last stages of her pregnancy, not be present at the birth of his child.

He said that on no account should she go to Windsor for her confinement. Heirs born in that grim grey castle were seldom lucky . . .

The marriage of Catherine of Valois to Henry V.

Catherine ignored this admonition and went to Windsor, bore her child there, a boy, destined to become Henry VI, a very unfortunate monarch indeed. To Henry, fighting in France the news came that his son was born. 'Where?', Henry asked. The messenger was obliged to say, 'Windsor', and the King sighed.

He was already in ill-health; like his grandfather, John of Gaunt, he had over-exerted himself. These campaigns which read so grandly, took toll even of the strongest; irregular, hurried meals, hard riding, battles, camps with their more deadly attacks upon the constitution. Henry V died young, only thirty-four, having reigned for nine years; his son, born at Windsor was then less than a year old.

Catherine had crossed to France and was with him when he died.

She was still only twenty, young enough and vigorous enough to do her mourning correctly and at the same time to see that her son was acknowledged as his father's heir. The long and disastrous wrangle between those who supported the House of Lancaster and those the House of York was about to resume. Perhaps she sensed it, for she took a great deal of trouble to put her son on show; she rode many miles in open litters with the child in her lap.

There were rules governing the re-marriage of kings' widows. Somehow Catherine evaded them all; she married, in such secrecy that no record

The birth of the ill-fated Henry VI at Windsor.

remains of when, or where, or by whom the ceremony was performed, a very obscure Welshman, a foot-soldier, not even a knight, Owen Tudor. He had fought with Henry V in France and acquitted himself so well that he had been made one of the King's personal body-guards, and as such he held a place in the household of the widowed Queen and the infant King.

Later on those who hated the Tudors said that this man's name was Tidder, and that his father had been a Welsh brewer; the pro-Tudor faction maintained that his name was Tudor and that he was descended from the great Welsh King, Cadwallader.

Catherine bore several children and one of them Henry VI acknowledged as his half-brother and made Earl of Richmond, and arranged a marriage for him to a girl who was in the Lancastrian line, a granddaughter of John of Gaunt. From this marriage came Henry Tudor, Henry VII. But that was all in the future.

Catherine died young, only thirty-five. She was given a splendid funeral; her son was not yet of full age, but he was King and the regents and relatives who governed him were prepared to defer to his wishes, at least in such minor things as his mother's burial in Westminster Abbey and the erection of a splendid alabaster memorial. It is part of the mystery which surrounds so much of her connection with the Tudors that her grandson, Henry VII, as soon as he came to the throne, had this memorial demolished.

Margaret of Anjou

Queen to Henry VI
born 1430, married 1445, died 1482

Margaret was born in 1430 in the middle of a civil war on the Continent, and was to spend much of her life waging civil war in England, in the deceptively named Wars of the Roses. It was not called by that name then – Sir Walter Scott, centuries later, christened it. While it was making so many people miserable it was known as the war between Lancaster and York; but the Lancastrians took a red rose as their emblem, and the Yorkists took a white one. It all hinged on which of Edward I's descendants had the better claim to the throne. Henry VI, tracing his lineage back to John of Gaunt, was Lancastrian; his rivals were a Duke of York, and then that Duke's son.

Margaret, though called Margaret of Anjou, was actually the daughter of the King of Sicily. Through her mother she could claim some of Charlemagne's blood. She needed it.

She was the subject of one of those cradle betrothals, so easily set aside. Then, still young, she was promised to young Henry of England, and at the age of fifteen, married to Henry who was twenty-four.

At the French Court, where she had received much of her education, Margaret had shown herself not only intelligent but precocious. She was pretty, animated, amiable; a most desirable bride. Henry's education had been entrusted to one of his uncles, the great Cardinal Beaufort; he was handsome, studious, courteous. In some respects they were well-matched, but she was made of sterner and more ruthless material than he was and he, dominated from earliest childhood by uncles and regents, was easily dominated by his vigorous, strong-minded wife who devoted her energies to keeping him on the throne, or restoring him to it.

Move by move, battle by battle, the Wars of the Roses make tedious reading. One thing is noticeable about it – it was less destructive to the economy and to the lives of ordinary people than former civil wars had

*The marriage of Margaret of Anjou to Henry VI, from a
contemporary manuscript.*

been because the feudal system had broken down and more people were in charge of their own destinies. Macaulay says that within a week the plough was back at work on what had been a battlefield; this was because the driver of the plough was no longer, as in earlier days, compelled to follow his liege lord into battle; the acres were his own, by purchase or leasehold and he had only to wait and then back to the plough. It was the same in towns, business as usual.

It was the great nobles who waged the war and who so weakened and impoverished themselves that when Henry Tudor – Lancastrian by birth, but neutral in conviction – came to the throne, he found the final subjugation of the barons who had caused his predecessors so much trouble a comparatively easy matter.

It was Queen Margaret who headed the Lancastrian forces. Henry VI was no soldier and he was already suffering intermittent fits of insanity. This malady he had inherited through his mother whose father, a King of France had had mad spells.

There had been a kind of general agreement, not unlike that between Matilda the Empress and her cousin Stephen, years ago; Henry VI of Lancaster was to hold the throne while he lived and Edward of York was to be his heir. But in 1453 Margaret gave birth to a son, Edward of Lancaster, and she had no intention of seeing his claim set aside.

She and her Lancastrian party enjoyed victories, suffered defeats. She is said to have been vindictive. When her party defeated the Duke of York near York itself, she is supposed to have ordered his dead body to hang from a prominent place, wearing a derisive paper crown.

The role of Amazon was more or less forced upon her, for when Henry VI was sane he was more interested in founding educational establishments; Eton College, intended to benefit a few indigent boys, and King's at Cambridge.

Despite all her efforts, battles, narrow escapes and hiding in forests, a visit to France to find allies from her kinsmen there, she was defeated. Her son was killed, at or after the battle of Tewkesbury which was a Yorkist victory. Her husband was put to death in the Tower of London and she was imprisoned there. A tigress in a cage.

Her French relatives who had done little to help her while she was active and able, did in the end use influence and she was allowed to go to France, there in the deepest seclusion to end her days. She lived to be fifty-one, missing by a mere three years the final triumph of the red rose of Lancaster over the white rose of York.

When she died, Edward IV ruled England, ably helped and supported by his brother Richard, Duke of Gloucester. The war seemed to be over and possibly Margaret – who had chosen as her emblem the simple, humble daisy – looked back from her seclusion and thought her years wasted. So much scheming, so much hardship, so much determination, all brought down to nothing. Since she lived in seclusion she probably did not see, but she must have heard about the Lancastrians in exile on the Continent. Edward had stripped them of their lands, distributed some estates amongst his followers, and kept so many for himself that he was the richest man in England. Edward's line seemed well established, he had an heir and another son. The Lancastrian cause seemed to be dead. But amongst the exiles, biding his time, was that Henry Tudor whose father Henry VI had created Earl of Richmond.

Katharine of Aragon, young and pensive as if she had a premonition of her future. A painting by Michael Sittow.

Regina Elizabetha consortis
Edwardi dei gracia Regis

Elizabeth Woodville

Queen to Edward IV
born 1437, married 1464, died 1492

No territorial claim here; she is described as an English gentlewoman; but her mother had been a princess of Luxembourg, and she herself had been one of Queen Margaret's ladies.

Many romantic stories are told about the meeting between Elizabeth and Edward; for hundreds of years there stood in the forest of Whittlebury a tree known as the Queen's Oak, under which she was said to have stood waiting to accost the King when he went hunting, and beg him to restore her dead husband's lands to her young sons.

It sounds feasible. Her husband had been an ardent Lancastrian, killed fighting against Edward, and Edward had confiscated estates belonging to Lancastrians. Also Edward was well known to have an eye for a pretty woman. Elizabeth Woodville must have had confidence in her beauty for she had had other suitors before Sir John Gray.

She was extremely fair, with silver-gilt hair, a milk-and-roses complexion. This is guesswork, but she was probably wearing mourning for her husband, and black is especially becoming to blondes.

What is certain is that Edward fell in love with her and tried to make her his mistress. Her reply to this proposal may be hearsay, but it fits the pattern; it is almost exactly what Anne Boleyn said to Henry VIII. 'My liege, I know I am not good enough to be your Queen, but I am far too good to be your mistress'.

They were married, but very secretly. Secretly because any man recently come to a throne was a marriage target for princesses and Edward wished not to offend anyone. But after about seven months during which rumour had mounted, Edward acknowledged her publicly as his wife and she had a splendid coronation.

A portrait of Elizabeth Woodville from a stained glass window in Canterbury Cathedral.

It was not only the foreign princesses and their sponsors who were offended; every marriageable woman of high birth and her relatives felt affronted. When a king married a princess naturally everybody understood, but when a king married a commoner, the widow of a mere knight, it caused some clamour in which 'Why not me? Why not mine?' figured largely.

It may have been this violent reaction against her that set Elizabeth about reinforcing her position by arranging marriages for all her kin, Woodville or Gray – one of them was extraordinary, the marriage of her eldest brother, a man in the prime of life, to the Dowager Duchess of Norfolk who was eighty.

Edward IV joined in this bolstering up process; he brought over from Luxembourg a number of people related to Elizabeth's mother, people with grand titles prepared to give the Queen of England the kiss of kinship and show to the world that she was not just the humble widow–woman that her enemies called her.

Their Court was very splendid and very gay and so extravagant that despite all he had taken from the Lancastrians, Edward was forced to impose heavy new taxes.

Elizabeth appears to have been a very feminine type of woman; she exercised a great deal of influence over the King, particularly in the early days of their marriage, but it was a kind of gossippy bedroom influence, aimed at making him favour her friends and dislike her enemies. She was occupied with arranging marriages, and bearing children – both feminine activities – and Edward never delegated any kind of power to her, even when he went abroad. This may have been because he realised that she had little capacity, or because he had such an excellent second-in-command in his brother, Richard of Gloucester.

One of the matches which Elizabeth arranged was that of her eldest daughter – another Elizabeth – with the eldest son of the King of France. This childhood betrothal was subsequently broken; perhaps because the King of France, keeping a close eye on England, and with many Lancastrian exiles around him, foresaw a day when an alliance with a Yorkist princess might not have the value that it seemed to have at present. Edward and Elizabeth were both much mortified by this breach of contract; in fact it was said to have had a bad effect upon Edward's health. It is possible; he came of a family well-known for fierce fits of temper; and a savage rage could injure a man, not yet old in years but who had lived hard in every sense of the word. He told somebody that he had fought in nine battles, in eight of them on foot. His reign had not been untroubled – one rebellion against him had been led by his brother, the Duke of Clarence. He loved his dear Elizabeth, and his marriage to her had cost him the allegiance of his most powerful subject; yet he found other women irresistible. He had crowded a lot of living into his forty-one years.

Edward died in 1483.

In his will he left no authority to his wife, except so far as the marriage of their daughters was concerned. He did, however use many affectionate expressions concerning her – the will was nine years old – and he left her well-provided for, except for the fact that most of what he bequeathed to her was land taken from the Lancastrians. So if the see-saw tipped again . . .

But why should it? There were Edward's two sons, mere children still, but there was their uncle, Richard of Gloucester, an able soldier and a good administrator. There were other uncles and relatives, all from her side of the family.

She was very feminine and there is that curious thing called feminine intuition; Elizabeth possessed it.

What else made her say, almost as soon as Edward IV was dead, that his heir, Edward V who was then in Ludlow Castle, should be brought to London immediately, *accompanied by a strong army*?

And why did she weep when her suggestion was pooh-poohed? The Lords of the Council thought it would be all wrong for the twelve-year-old King to come to his capital with an armed guard. Against whom must he be guarded? Who were his enemies?

So the young King set out from Ludlow attended only by the ordinary retinue which included two of his uncles from his mother's side of the family; and his uncle, Richard of Gloucester, who was in the North at the time of Edward IV's death, turned south and intercepted the unarmed convoy. That the King's uncles, members of Elizabeth's much-hated family should be arrested was no surprise. The young King was taken as well and lodged in the Tower of London, but not in the prison part of it; in the palace part.

So far Elizabeth had had no reason to suspect Richard of Gloucester of any ill-intention towards the young King, his nephew. Richard had had him publicly proclaimed as Edward V at York; and he had written Elizabeth a kind letter of condolence upon the loss of her husband. So why did she take fright again, and hurry her second son, the Duke of York and all her daughters into sanctuary in Westminster Abbey?

(This idea of a holy place offering immunity even to a known criminal was very ancient. In theory, anybody, however guilty, if he could get into a church and lay hold of the altar could not be arrested in the ordinary way. Hunger and thirst might force him out into the open, so could fire, and over the years the belief that any sanctified place was a refuge had become rather a stylised form than an actuality.)

Elizabeth – intuitive again – saw that while her second son, Richard, Duke of York, aged eleven, was alive, it would be worth nobody's while to do away with his brother. So why did she hand the younger boy over?

Of all the complicated histories of Queens this is surely the most confused. There was the question of sanctuary. It was pointed out to this poor distracted woman that while sanctuary must be offered to men and women it could not well apply to children who could not be held guilty of any crime. There was the plea that young Edward V was lonely in the Tower and would appreciate his brother's company. And there was the fact that Richard of Gloucester had now been proclaimed Lord Protector of the Realm, and had fixed his young nephew's coronation day.

She let him go and he, with his brother, King but never crowned, simply vanished.

Some most entertaining books have been written, doing white-washing jobs on Richard III, but some things stick out of the white-wash. He employed agents to go about London, getting up a petition by which the citizens begged Richard to become King, a long minority rule being bad for the country. And there was an attempt to prove that all Edward IV's children were illegitimate because he had been betrothed to another lady before he married Elizabeth. Betrothals were always the jokers in the pack.

Those who exonerate Richard III from all blame for the death of the two young Princes in the Tower, point to the apparently amiable relationship which existed between him and the boys' mother. Would any woman, they ask, be on friendly terms with the murderer of her sons? It is an argument, but it ignores facts which may sound sordid, but were influential. She had other children, five daughters; and she could not keep herself, and them, in sanctuary at Westminster forever. Sanctuary meant just what it said, protection; it did not guarantee any form of service, or even a regular supply of food. She gave in, was moved to another part of Westminster and suffered the humiliation of seeing herself described as Dame Gray, lately calling herself Queen of England.

Richard, who is said to have idolised his elder brother, was probably one of those who did not think Dame Gray a suitable wife for him; he certainly disliked all her kin, both Woodvilles and Grays.

Elizabeth spent the two years of Richard's reign in obscurity and under some form of control; but she lived to see happier days. Henry Tudor came out of exile, defeated the Yorkists finally in the battle of Bosworth and chose Elizabeth of York – she who might have been Queen of France – for his bride. He was a dutiful son-in-law; he restored the Queen Dowager's lands and ordered that the document by which she was deprived of them should be burnt. When his first son, Arthur, was christened in Winchester Cathedral Elizabeth was there, not only as the child's grandmother but as his god-mother, too. She went to live, as a guest, not as a nun, in Bermondsey convent, but was at Court for any very special occasion, once at least taking the place of her daughter who had just had another child. So dignity was restored to her before she died.

Anne
of Warwick

Queen to Richard III
born 1456, married 1472, died 1485

She was Queen of England very briefly – only two years – but her story is very crowded and very colourful.

She was the second daughter of that great Earl of Warwick, known as the Kingmaker because he was so rich and so powerful that the side he supported in the Lancaster–York squabble was usually successful; for a time.

Warwick aimed to be a Queenmaker too, and when Anne was fourteen she was married to the Prince of Wales, the son of Henry VI and Margaret of France. He was killed at or shortly after the battle of Tewkesbury. The stories vary. What is certain is that she was a widow at fifteen, the widow of a Lancastrian prince, in an England controlled by the Yorkists.

Most stories coincide about her working as a kitchen-maid in a mean London house; but the reasons given for this masquerade differ.

The Earl of Warwick had obviously performed that action known as hedging one's bets; he had married Anne to the Lancastrian Prince of Wales, and his other daughter, Isabel, to a Yorkist, the Duke of Clarence, brother to Edward IV. So some stories say that Clarence, not wishing to share his wife's inheritance with her sister, forced Anne into disguise and kitchen work; others say that she voluntarily hid herself because she did not wish to marry Richard, Duke of Gloucester.

However, marry him she did, at Westminster in 1472.

After that she and Richard spent most of their time in the north of England. Richard showed by his subsequent behaviour how much he disliked his brother Edward's Queen and all her clan; he loved his brother but was seldom seen at a Court thronging with Woodvilles and Grays.

At Middleham Castle, in Yorkshire, Anne bore a child – a boy, named Edward.

*The ruins of Middleham Castle, where Anne of Warwick spent
much of her time with Richard III after their marriage.*

When Richard of Gloucester succeeded his brother – and whether
Edward's sons were then dead or merely shuffled aside will probably remain
a question with no answer – Anne came south and shared his coronation at
Westminster and her small son was acknowledged as Prince of Wales.

There was a second coronation; in York. Richard III, whatever his vices
or virtues, did in this second coronation show an awareness of a division in
England, not marked on any map; the North was the North and the South
was the South; even the English they spoke was different. So in the cause of
unity, he organised this second coronation.

Then her son, her only child, died in March 1484; they called it 'a rapid
decline', probably one of those diseases that lay in ambush for the young.

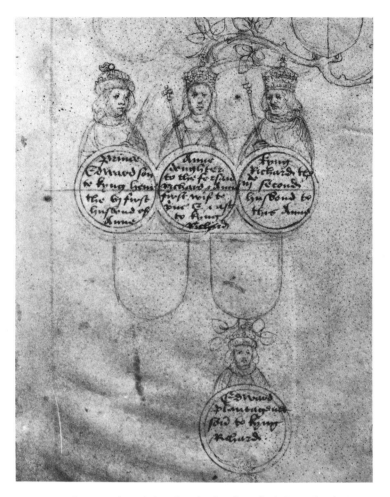

Anne of Warwick with her first husband on the left, Richard III
on the right, and their only child Edward, from the Beauchamp
Pageant, 1480–85.

It could have been an inherited tuberculosis, for almost immediately Anne of Warwick also suffered a decline in health, not rapid; it took her a year to die.

She died before the decisive battle of Bosworth; so she was still Queen and entitled to a grand funeral in Westminster Abbey. If, as some people believe, she hated Richard she did not live to see him overthrown; if, as another theory holds, she was devoted to him, she was spared the knowledge that he was dead, and the crown which he had worn outside his helmet had fallen into a hawthorn bush, from which it was retrieved and set upon the head of Henry Tudor.

Elizabeth of York

Queen to Henry VII
born 1466, married 1486, died 1503

The last princess of the Yorkist line and the first of the Tudor Queens, Elizabeth was born in the Palace of Westminster early in 1466. She inherited her mother's fair colouring. Until the death of her father, Edward IV, she lived a secure and happy life. Elizabeth Woodville's strong family feeling towards those connected to her by birth or marriage, seems to have been passed on to her own family. All Elizabeth Woodville's daughters – except Elizabeth who was then Queen, and who was in child-bed – were by her death-bed; and when she died and could no longer provide from her Queen Dowager's revenue for her four unmarried daughters, Elizabeth assumed responsibility for them.

Being so fond of her sisters, how did Elizabeth feel about the disappearance of those two young brothers? There is no answer.

Henry VII, the first Tudor King of England, has come down in history as a miser and his best-known portrait shows his face as solemn and humourless, slightly grim. But like all other men, he had been young, and was more of a soldier than an accountant. He was twenty-nine when he became King, and he married Elizabeth of York in the next year. They had a magnificent coronation. All but a few stubborn dissidents were delighted to have the long civil war over and Lancaster and York united in marriage. Henry put the two roses, the red and white together in that famous symbol of unity, the Tudor Rose. The early years of Henry's reign were not untroubled; his sensible conviction that the recent civil war had been caused by nobles with too much power, led him to forbid the maintenance of private armies. Lords who hated this reduction of their power, supported two rather futile little rebellions.

Elizabeth and Henry both understood the value of the marriage game as it was played in their day. For Arthur, Prince of Wales they chose a Spanish

A rather stylised portrait of Elizabeth of York by an unknown artist.

princess, Katharine of Aragon; and their daughter Margaret could be usefully married to the King of Scotland. For their second son Henry – destined to be one of the most married men in history – they planned no marriage at all. He was very clever; he must be a cleric; Archbishop of Canterbury? Cardinal? And their second daughter, Mary? Perhaps Queen of France.

Katharine of Aragon, somewhat older than Arthur, did eventually come to England and was married. Henry VII, now grown close-fisted, opened that fist and gave the young couple a wedding to supersede all weddings. Within five months Arthur was dead. He and Katharine were then at Ludlow Castle – the usual residence of Princes of Wales – and why and how he died

*Henry VII's miserliness, solemnity and lack of humour is very
evident in this painting, possibly by Michael Sittow.
He holds a Tudor rose in his hand.*

has never been made very clear. There was the sweating sickness in Ludlow
at the time; it was also said that while overheated, he drank ice-cold water.

Arthur had always been frail and pale and now he was dead; and it is
about this death that Henry and Elizabeth stand out most clearly as people.
They 'shared their painful grief', and Elizabeth reminded Henry that he
was not entirely bereft; he still had a son – Henry. Her behaviour to Henry
and his to her during their mutual sorrow, indicates that their marriage was
happy; none of her enemies, and none of his, ever flung out a hint of
infidelity on either side.

Elizabeth died young, in 1503 on the very day of her thirty-seventh
birthday. She may have been another victim to tuberculosis, then known
by the apt name of consumption. There is a tenuous connection between
the disease and brilliantly fair complexions, and a less tenuous one between
it and child-bearing; four of her children are remembered, but she bore
seven.

Henry the miser proved open-handed again. She had a fine funeral as a
good Queen deserved. Her body was embalmed and lay in state in the
Tower of London, not far from the place where her two young brothers,
by whomever murdered, had been hastily shovelled away.

She went to her grave leaving behind her a husband, not yet fifty, still an
eligible man, and a son of twelve, but unlike his brother Arthur, very strong,
very precocious . . .

Katharine
of Aragon

First Queen to Henry VIII
born 1486, married 1509, died 1536
See colour plate facing page 80.

Katharine, a most pious, orthodox Catholic was to a degree responsible for bringing the Reformation to England. No one woman before or after, ever gave, unintentionally, such a twist to history.

She was the daughter of Ferdinand of Aragon and Isabella of Castile whose marriage made Spain one country, and whose efforts drove the Moors – Moslems – out of that corner of Spain known as Granada.

Proud, fifteen years old, with the vast dowry which her parents thought suitable for a princess of Spain, she came to England and married Arthur, Prince of Wales. Henry VII gave the young couple a most magnificent wedding. Every conduit in London spouted wine. Then they went off to Ludlow, the residence of the Prince of Wales, and there Arthur died.

Presently a whole slab of history was to balance precariously upon the simple question of whether this marriage had been consummated or not. Katharine to the end said, No; she and Arthur had lived, very fondly, but as brother and sister.

While Elizabeth of York lived, Katharine was treated as the widow of the Prince of Wales; later on she was to live, with undiminished dignity, through some hard times, often so ill-provided for that she was dependent upon the Spanish Ambassador for wine and similar small luxuries.

Henry VII's avarice had got the better of him and Katharine was one outstanding victim of the dowry-and-marriage-settlement system. She had brought half her huge dowry with her and if she returned to Spain, as her parents originally requested, that half dowry would have to be returned. And, perhaps worse, the income from the estates settled on her as Princess of Wales, would also be lost to England. Henry hated the idea and eventually found what he thought a solution. Katharine should marry Henry, now heir apparent, six years her junior.

*Henry VIII as he doubtless liked to be portrayed; virile and
arrogant – the master of women as well as the State. A painting by Holbein.*

*Katherine of Aragon looks even sadder in this portrait than in
the painting of her as a girl facing page 80.*

Katharine wrote to her father that she had no wish to make a second
marriage in England, but would of course bow to his wish, and up came that
old delusionary bugbear to which so many princesses were sacrificed.
Ferdinand did wish for a firm alliance with England because now he was
at war with France.

More than a father-in-law's scheming and a father's consent were necessary to bring this marriage about. The Church held even stronger views
about marrying deceased spouses' husbands and wives than it did about
marriages between cousins; but, given the right amount of diplomacy and
some pressure, a Papal dispensation could be obtained. Katharine's mother,
the redoubtable Isabella, may have had doubts, but she was sick, a worn-out
woman, and news that the dispensation had been granted, reached her when
she was dying.

Katharine, now eighteen, was once again betrothed to a Prince of Wales –
that handsome, well-grown, precocious boy who had led her to the altar
when she married Arthur. Perhaps Henry VII was aware of his son's precocity

and strongly sexual nature, for as soon as the betrothal was made he took great pains to keep Katharine and Henry apart. Once indeed, with the political wind shifting, he thought of disregarding this betrothal altogether and marrying his son elsewhere, but nothing came of that; and how Henry felt about Katharine is made fairly plain by the fact that he married her as soon as the conventional period of mourning for his father was ended; how she felt about him is made more than plain in her last letter.

Their first child was a daughter, and Henry VIII's reception of the news that Katharine had borne a girl, not a boy, contradicts the image that has come down to us, an ogrish tyrant. He welcomed his daughter, said, 'There will be other children', and proudly carried the little girl about, showing her off to courtiers and ambassadors.

After Mary's birth, Katharine's child-bearing story is a story of calamity; miscarriages; still-born children; a boy who lived only a few weeks.

Apart from this – most vital – side to it, their marriage was happy. Both were scholarly, and their glittering Court was the cultural centre of Europe. Henry was unfaithful; Katharine ignored his infidelities, and one of his bastards – a handsome boy – came to Court and was accepted by the Queen. In fact she would accept anything from him except divorce.

It is not impossible that Henry eventually did come to look upon his marriage as cursed – as set down in the Bible in the Book of Deuteronomy; up to a point he was pious; all those pregnancies and still no heir. His doubts about his marriage would have sounded more sincere had he not at the time been infatuated by one of Katharine's waiting women, Anne Boleyn whose attitude was exactly that of Elizabeth Woodville – 'I am too good to be your mistress'; but even that does not convict him of complete hypocrisy.

Henry offered Katharine anything she cared to name if only she would agree to a divorce, admitting that their marriage had been illegal from the beginning. It was like arguing with rock; she swore that she had never been Arthur's wife in the carnal sense; she argued that the Pope had allowed her marriage to Henry, and only the Pope could dissolve it; she argued that to admit the illegality of the marriage would be to make Mary, their daughter, a bastard.

The King lost patience, banished his Queen from Court, took away the Crown Jewels, did not allow her to see her daughter. She complied, with meekness but with dignity, to every move made against her. She had faith in the Pope and in the Emperor Charles V who was her nephew. Neither lifted a finger to help her, until it was too late.

She heard about Henry's throwing off the Pope's command over the Church in England; heard of his marriage to Anne Boleyn; the birth of his daughter Elizabeth. But she never wavered, and dying in Kimbolton Castle, grey and cold, she wrote Henry a love-letter . . . and signed it 'Katharine, the Queen'.

Anne Boleyn

Second Queen to Henry VIII
born about 1507, married 1533, died 1536

Who was this girl – possibly the best-known of all England's Queen con-
sorts – who held out against Henry, who thought forward and said any
child she bore must be acknowledged, and whose child was Elizabeth I?

On her mother's side she was related to the Howards who were Dukes of
Norfolk; on her father's side she was related to the up-and-coming Boleyns,
typical of their time, men who had married well, or done well in business.

When she was born, she was so unimportant that even her birthplace is
disputable; Blicking Hall in Norfolk? Hever Castle in Kent? And exactly
when? Nobody bothered to note.

What we do know about her is that when Henry VII succeeded in marrying his younger daughter, Mary, to the ageing King of France, Anne Boleyn
went with her, a very young lady-in-waiting. And when the King of France
died, and Mary Tudor married, without consulting her royal brother of
England, one of his lords, and came home in disgrace, Anne Boleyn came
with her – or shortly afterwards – and was given a place amongst Queen
Katharine's women.

She is one of the few women whom no chronicler describes as fair; some
say she was downright plain, sallow, black-haired and black-eyed. She
suffered two other physical drawbacks; a huge mole, the size of a strawberry
on her neck, and on her left hand, an extra small finger. But she had that
indefinable thing called style; even her ways of disguising her defects were
so stylish that other ladies, with no moles on their necks, took to wearing
necklaces like dog-collars; ladies with the normal number of fingers had
their sleeves made extra long to dangle over the hands.

She had charm, too; many men loved her.

Around the Court at the time when she was a lady-in-waiting, was young
Lord Henry Percy, heir to the Earl of Northumberland. He fell in love with

her, and she with him. But Henry VIII had become aware of her fascination. He had a little talk with his great minister of state, Cardinal Wolsey, who sent the young man's father the unwelcome news that his heir was contemplating making a highly unsuitable marriage. The Earl came storming down from the North, informed Lord Henry that he was already betrothed to a lady of his own rank, and took him away.

The King was by this time an experienced seducer and knew that clandestine affairs were more easily conducted away from Court; so Anne was sent home to Hever Castle, to spend a dull time in the company of her stepmother, a good woman of humble origin, not calculated to be much company for a girl accustomed to Court life. Her father and her brother were too busy fostering their own varying interests to spend much time at home. Henry thought that his visits would be welcome.

They were not; Anne was sullen, cool, evasive. Ordered to play the lute, or to sing for the King, she did so, but she gave no sign that she was flattered, or even interested in his attentions. Her behaviour simply whetted his appetite and one day he begged her to become his mistress.

Anne knew what happened to mistresses – her sister Mary, utterly unlike her in every way – had been one of Henry's. Mistresses were abandoned as soon as the man's fancy waned. She said with perfect frankness that she would be Queen or nothing. This did not deter Henry. In fact he remained so deeply infatuated with her, and for so long a time, that people muttered darkly about witchcraft. What else could account for it?

Henry told Wolsey to set about getting a divorce on the grounds that his marriage to Katharine, his dead brother's wife, was an offence to God. Wolsey failed. The Pope could argue, justly, that his predecessor had granted a dispensation for the marriage and that what one Pope had given another could not withdraw. So Wolsey, who had served Henry faithfully and well, was disgraced, stripped of wealth and power and would have faced impeachment had he not died on his way to London. By a coincidence which no novelist would have dared to use, it was Henry Percy, now Earl of Northumberland who was entrusted with the duty of bringing the old, heart-broken man to London.

Punishing Wolsey was not enough; the Pope was the real offender. Henry moved against him, too. He ordered that England should be free of all Papal rule. He himself would be head of the church – but a church almost unchanged in any other way. Henry was very far from being a Protestant; but, free of Rome he could choose 'his own Archbishop of Canterbury – Cranmer – who declared that Henry's marriage to Katharine was null and void and that he was free to marry Anne.

The attitude of the people towards all this was curiously ambivalent; many men were glad to be freed of the Papal dues, the Peter's pence, a penny a year on every fireplace in a house, and various other dues. But this feeling

Anne Boleyn by an unknown artist.

was offset by sympathy with Queen Katharine and a dislike of Anne personally – the snob element which had operated against Elizabeth Wood-ville. They shouted in the streets that they did not want Nan Bullen as Queen, and the de-grandising of her name was the measure of their disgust.

Anne had a secret, private wedding; and there was good reason for it. As soon as she realised that Henry was serious in his intention of marrying her at whatever cost, she had at last yielded, and was pregnant. So the fewer people who knew about the exact date of the wedding, the better.

Had she given Henry an heir, she might have lived longer. A daughter first; accepted much as the King had accepted Mary – a promise of things to come. Then Anne miscarried, late enough in the pregnancy for male characteristics to be visible in the embryo. She was no fool; she summed up the situation in six words; 'I have miscarried of my saviour'. But, far-sighted as she was she could hardly, one thinks, foresee the end of the road for which this miscarriage was the beginning. At the worst she could have only anticipated divorce.

It was her misfortune that divorce was a word Henry was heartily sick of. He accused Anne of adultery – in a Queen an act of treason.

Unless she, a clear-headed woman who had proved, by her holding off of Henry's wooing, to have her sexual impulses well in hand, had gone

*Hever Castle, Kent, the charming Tudor house where Anne
Boleyn was brought up.*

raving mad, would she have committed adultery with no fewer than five
men, one her paid musician, and one her own brother? That was the charge
brought against her – and against them.

She was Queen of England and must be tried by her peers – amongst
whom was her first love, a sick man who had refused to honour the betrothal
his father had made for him, and who died unmarried.

As a concession to the position she once held, she was beheaded not by a
clumsy axe, but by a sword, wielded by a skilled man, brought over from
France. Informed of this, and the assurance that there would be hardly any
pain, she said, with a flash of the old spirit, 'I have heard that the executioner
is very good. And I have a little neck'.

Her last message to Henry, unlike Katharine's which was so loving, was
sardonic.

She was beheaded on Friday, 19 May 1536, and buried, we are told, in
an old arrow box, too short to accommodate her – she was rather tall –
without her severed head lying beside her. But there are other stories,
conflicting with the account that she was buried in the Tower Precincts.
During her life-time she made enemies, but she also made friends, and these
friends are said to have conveyed her body, secretly, to a more suitable
resting place; under a plain, unmarked marble slab in a Norfolk church,
near her birthplace. The patron of the church will not allow the slab to be
lifted and the church is said to be haunted.

Jane Seymour

Third Queen to Henry VIII
born about 1506, married 1536, died 1537

Henry VIII, finely dressed, well-mounted, was awaiting the signal gun which would declare him a free man again. When it sounded, at mid-day, he shouted, 'Loose the hounds and away!'

His destination was Wolf Hall in Wiltshire. He had already chosen his next wife, and while five young men on 18 May and Anne on the next day were suffering and facing death, the hearths and ovens at Wolf Hall had been busy preparing for his betrothal to Jane, to be celebrated on the twentieth. They were married in Whitehall ten days later.

Jane Seymour was the eldest daughter of Sir John Seymour, an ordinary country gentleman; but Jane had been at Court, serving Anne Boleyn as Anne had served Katharine of Aragon; and there the King had noticed her – a meek, unobtrusive young woman, no longer a girl, and as great a contrast to Anne as Anne had been to Katharine. There is, in fact, about all Henry's marriages an element of rebound.

Jane was married, but her coronation was postponed. It was summer and the minor plagues were rampant. And then she was pregnant.

She was thirty-three, even in these days of pre-natal care and medical knowledge just a *trifle* late for a first parturition. Jane had an agonising time but at the end produced what she, the King and the whole country wanted – a Prince. He was born on Friday, 12 October 1537 at Hampton Court, the palace which had once been Wolsey's. It happened to be the eve of St Edward's day, and five Kings of England had borne the name of Edward, so he was baptized by that name on Monday 14 October. It was a ceremony of great splendour in which both Edward's half-sisters played their part. Mary was twenty-one years old and Elizabeth was four. Both had been declared bastards and Mary had infuriated Henry by her refusal to acknowledge that her mother's marriage to him had been invalid. Elizabeth was too

Jane Seymour – meek and unobtrusive. Painter unknown.

young to have given any offence, but she was the daughter of a woman beheaded for treason. Yet, in this superb moment, all was forgiven. (Amongst his other inconsistencies of character, Henry had a strong paternal streak.)

Typical of the times was the fact that also present by the font of solid silver and playing his part in the ceremony, was the father of Anne Boleyn and of George Boleyn. Sentiment was a luxury few could afford.

The ceremony had begun in Queen Jane's bed-chamber where she was lifted on to a kind of sofa, upon which, wrapped in suitable robes, she was carried to the chapel – no great distance. But the ceremony lasted a long time and next day she was very ill. In a fortnight she was dead.

As a step-mother she had endeared herself to the Princess Mary who acted as chief mourner at her elaborate funeral which took place at Windsor.

Henry who hated any sign of mourning wore black until early in the following year. But he was soon looking around for another wife.

Anne
of Cleves

Fourth Queen to Henry VIII
born 1515, married 1540, died 1557

It took Henry two years to find himself another wife. One lady to whom he offered his hand summed up the situation when she said tartly that if she had two heads she would risk it, having only one she dare not.

Eventually one of Henry's agents found, at the Court of the Duke of Cleves, two sisters. Anne was the younger and the prettier.

(It is a curious comment upon the changing styles of what is regarded as beauty, that when the portraits of all Henry's Queens are compared, Anne is much the best looking – to modern eyes, at least.)

In her favour was her religion; Cleves was part of the Protestant part of Europe, and England, despite all Henry's efforts to hold to the middle line, was becoming more Protestant every day.

Anne had been strictly brought up; not well-educated, except in the use of the needle, but was said to have a good wit and the ability to learn. Henry decided to marry her, sent over a suitable escort and at home made preparations for her reception which was to be magnificent. The solemn contract of marriage was signed at Düsseldorf in October 1539, there was a marriage by proxy, and everywhere in her long slow journey towards England, Anne was addressed as Queen; in England Henry spoke of her as his spouse and arranged for her coronation to take place early in the following year. She landed at Deal and the King went as far as Rochester to meet her.

He took a dislike to her at first sight; he spoke of her as a 'great Flanders mare', and was furious with all who had recommended her to him. He did not think that he was no longer quite the handsome young man that he had once been; he was forty-six, and, during his married life with Anne Boleyn, had been unhorsed in a tournament and received a wound on his shin which never completely healed; unable to exercise as much as formerly he was growing fat, as many retired athletes do.

Anne had the good wit enough not to oppose his proposal to divorce her – but to treat her as an honoured sister. It is more than likely that she herself pointed to a way out of the impasse. There had been rumours, during the marriage negotiations, that she had formerly been betrothed, but her family had firmly denied them. She probably remembered.

This, Henry's second divorce, gave no trouble at all. There was no need to consult the Pope; by July the whole thing was amicably arranged. Anne was to take precedence of everyone at Court – except the King's two daughters and any woman he might marry; she was assured of an income of £500 a year – at that time a more than comfortable sum. Anne wrote to her brother – who had succeeded her father, 'The King's highness whom I cannot have as a husband is nevertheless a most kind, loving and friendly father and brother'. She expressed no wish, never made an attempt, to return to her native land; she said she was content.

She loved fine clothes and now had plenty of them. She enjoyed the company of Henry's daughters and sometimes that of the King himself. She saw Henry's fifth marriage come to grief, and his sixth end with his death. She saw his son's brief reign, and actually made her last public appearance at the coronation of his daughter Mary, on which occasion she rode in the same carriage as the Queen's sister, the Princess Elizabeth.

Anne died in 1557, of some unspecified 'declining' illness. She left a remarkable will in which almost everyone who had ever served her in however humble a capacity was remembered.

Some theorists believe that there is a chemical element in sexual attraction; it may have been at work here, in both Henry and Anne; instant repudiation upon his side, placid acceptance of the situation on hers. Otherwise, for Anne was young when she came to England, she might have borne strong sons – but then England would never have had Elizabeth I.

Anne was buried, with all due honour, at Westminster.

Anne of Cleves: the portrait by Holbein sent to Henry VIII at the sight of which he proceeded with the marriage negotiations.

Catherine Howard

Fifth Queen to Henry VIII
born about 1522, married 1540, died 1542

This is such a romantic, dramatic, confused story and it has been so much written about that one hardly dares offer it again.

Catherine was Anne Boleyn's cousin, and, like her, step-granddaughter of the Duchess of Norfolk. While she was still young her mother died and the girl was handed over to her grandmother's care and reared in what, even for Tudor times, was a remarkably ramshackle household. Admittedly the Duchess, when she stumbled across her granddaughter and Sir Francis Dereham embracing each other, struck him, beat Catherine, and for good measure dealt a blow or two to the attendant who should have prevented such behaviour, but what went on out of her sight she seemed not to care about.

In the Duchess's various great houses the child shared a kind of dormitory with waiting-women, not all of good character and one of whom actively encouraged her first, precocious *affaire* with Henry Mannox, a man of low status, a hired musician. It may have been part of his duty to teach Catherine to play upon the virginals. She was musical and many young girls do fall in love with their music teachers. Her other lover was Sir Francis Dereham, a distant relative. He is said to have ingratiated himself by giving her a piece of finery – an artificial flower. Catherine had no money with which to buy such things; the Duchess felt that she had done her duty in providing board and lodging.

Bacchanalian scenes took place in some of those long, ill-lit rooms; men were smuggled in, bringing food and wine with them.

The Duchess of Norfolk, so little concerned for Catherine's moral well-being, was not one to miss a chance of advancing her in the world, and when Anne of Cleves' Flemish attendants went home, Catherine was introduced to her household as a lady-in-waiting. There the King saw her and fell in

A miniature of Catherine Howard probably painted by Holbein,
1540–41. 'The King is so amorous of Catherine Howard that
he cannot treat her well enough and caresses her more than he did
the others.'

love. Despite his bad record as a husband, there is something slightly pathetic about this infatuation. He was ageing – marriage to a young girl would renew his youth. And it might produce another son.

The date of Catherine's birth is unknown, but peripheral evidence goes to show that she could not have been more than eighteen, and may have been even younger, when she became Queen of England. She and Henry were married very quietly at Oatlands, in Surrey on 28 July.

It sounds extraordinary but Henry could not afford to give his fifth Queen a coronation. He had inherited a fortune from his miserly father, but it was spent; keeping up with Francis of France at such shows as the Field of the Cloth of Gold had cost a fortune; building ships for the Royal Navy was an expensive hobby, and only a year earlier Henry had spent a great deal of money on preparations for Anne of Cleves.

Impartial observers attributed the lack of ceremonial to the King's wish to be alone as much as possible with his young bride. Even in public, men noted, he was more free with loving gestures towards her than he had been to any other wife.

Most writers refer to her as small, as young. Some say she was beautiful; others that she had more grace than beauty. Grace had been the most distinguishing thing about her cousin, Anne Boleyn.

Henry called her his 'Rose without a Thorn', and possibly even then he was remembering Anne Boleyn, with her sharp wit and her cutting tongue.

The marriage had not been popular. Another commoner – and a Catholic at that! Catherine had hardly been publicly acknowledged before tongues were wagging. What of her past? Henry took no notice beyond having two men known to have said disparaging things consigned to the dungeons at Windsor. But Catherine *had* a past and it crept up on her. There is a sinister smack of blackmail about some of her household appointments. Two women given posts were those who had shared those indecorous romps, and her musician was Henry Mannox; her private secretary was Sir Francis Dereham. She also entertained privately and gave gifts to a cousin of hers, Thomas Culpepper.

Whether she was or was not guilty of adultery – and therefore treason – nobody can now decide. If she did admit another man to her bed she must have been mad – she knew what had happened to Anne Boleyn.

Much of the evidence against her was obviously rigged. She was said to have written many incriminating love-letters – to whom? None was ever produced, and her education had been so neglected that she could barely sign her name.

It is *just* possible that her early seduction had given rise to a condition now known as nymphomania and that it had induced her to take incredible risks; but she denied to the bitter end that she had ever betrayed the King. And there is a smack of truth about Sir Francis Dereham's evidence when he was examined; he said that a promise of marriage had been exchanged between them when she had been in the Duchess of Norfolk's care and he in the Duchess's service; they had called one another husband and wife and he had given her money when he had it; but he denied absolutely that there had been the slightest familiarity between them once she was Queen.

There is some integrity, too, in Catherine's refusal to take the easy way out which a previous marital arrangement with Dereham offered; Anne of Cleves had gone out by that comfortable door. But Catherine denied any formal contract.

It had all begun with gossip which Henry had at first ignored and then heeded. Why? The whole affair shows signs of haste and contrivance; one day the King and Queen were at Hampton Court together, taking the Sacrament in preparation for the celebration of All Souls' Day, and Henry was thanking God for the good life he was living with his loving, amiable, and virtuous wife, and almost on the next day he was accepting – in a passion of tears – some far from conclusive evidence of her infidelity.

There is a school of thought which holds that Henry VIII had in his youth suffered from syphilis, new to Europe; said to have been brought by the Portuguese from Africa, or by the Spaniards from America. It would account for all Katharine of Aragon's miscarriages and for the pallor and ill-health of his three surviving children; it would account for that ulcer on his shin which never healed. It would also account for his peculiar behaviour over Catherine, for syphilis, apparently cured, a thing of the past, an illness forgotten, can crop up in later years as damage to the brain.

Henry's behaviour was remarkably inconsistent. He wept when told what gossip was saying; yet, although they were still under the same roof, he made no attempt to face his wife with the rumours, or to hear what she had to say; he simply hurried away from Hampton Court, leaving everything to Archbishop Cranmer who could hardly help being prejudiced against Catherine on account of her religion.

It was not a case of Anne Boleyn's story being repeated; Henry had wished to be rid of her because he had fallen in love with Jane Seymour. He had no such reason for wishing to be rid of Catherine. He must have known what another wife-execution would do to his reputation. He was laying himself open to scorn and ridicule, and to the humiliation of receiving from his old rival, Francis of France, a letter of false condolence, commiserating with him over 'the naughty demeanour' of his wife.

Henry, in his youth, had studied to be a churchman, which meant some training in law; he knew as well as any man what was admissible evidence and what was not, and he was well aware of the opening which a pre-contract offered – it had worked well with Anne of Cleves. Yet he pressed on towards the travesty of a trial, even when Catherine did admit that at Horsham she and Francis Dereham had kissed and half in joke been called husband and wife. She still denied any formal betrothal, but in a crisis the use of those words, before witnesses, would have been considered sufficient.

Catherine was moved from Hampton Court to Sion House and confined to two rooms hung 'with mean stuff'. Anne Boleyn had been allowed to speak in her own defence, Catherine was not, possibly because Anne's speech had been so witty and eloquent.

When first accused, Catherine had fallen into such a fit of frenzy that those with her thought that she might die; but she recovered and apart from tears, appeared to be calm.

Trial by torture, if not actually illegal, had fallen into disuse in England; but there are indications that it was used to extract confessions from Francis Dereham and Thomas Culpepper; 'nothing more could be got out of him', has a sinister tone, and one of Dereham's friends had all his teeth forced out in the effort to make him remember conversations – the gist of which was that Dereham had said that he wished to marry Catherine but dared not because the King was beginning to love her.

*Traitor's Gate, the Tower of London, even in sunlight and
today, still retains its sinister appearance.*

Both Dereham and Culpepper were found guilty of treason and executed
at Tyburn. Dereham suffered the long-drawn-out death, he was hanged,
drawn and quartered; Culpepper, because of his closer relationship with the
Howards, was simply beheaded; but both their heads were exhibited, on
spikes, on Tower Bridge.

Catherine was beheaded within the Tower, at the same place and on the
same block as Anne Boleyn. She did not go alone; executed with her was
the wife of Anne's brother George, Lady Rochford, who, so few years
before, had been the chief instigator of the charge of incest between her
husband and her sister-in-law. Now she lost her head because she was
accused of conniving at Catherine's acts of infidelity. About her fate there
was a kind of rough justice; about Catherine's little of any kind.

Her ghost is said to walk a certain gallery in Hampton Court.

Katharine Parr

Sixth Queen to Henry VIII
born about 1512, married 1543, died 1548

In the old days when such things were learned by rote, anyone who struggled successfully through the list of Henry's Queens always ended 'Katharine Parr, who survived him'. Few people realise that she had a very narrow escape, if not from death, from Henry's displeasure, which was still formidable. It is a misconception to think of Henry's last marriage as a placid, Darby-and-Joan affair or of Katharine as an elderly woman, fit mate for an ageing man. She was thirty when she married him; he was fifty-two. What makes her sound so middle-aged is the fact that she had already been widowed twice. Both her former husbands had been elderly men, and both had left her considerable fortunes. She was on the point of marrying a third time, this time the most handsome, sought-after man in England, Thomas Seymour, when the King indicated that his young brother-in-law would be well advised to back away.

She was a woman of spirit. When Henry first made his intention to marry her plain she told him that it was better to be his mistress than his wife. Such frank criticism of his record as a husband did not anger the King, it increased his ardour.

Katharine had a proper wedding in the chapel of Hampton Court. Both Henry's daughters were present – to them and to the little Prince Edward, Katharine was to prove a good step-mother; she had experience in that role. And in the managing of old, irritable men.

The *average* life span in Tudor times was less than it is today but that must not be taken to mean that *individuals* could not reach a ripe old age in full possession of their physical and mental faculties. Henry was fifty-two – many men older than that fathered children, and Katharine was still well within the child-bearing age. But no child came of this marriage, though Henry plainly hoped. He expressed his wish, and Parliament endorsed it, that any children she bore him should be next in succession after Edward. Had she had even a daughter it would have pushed Mary and Elizabeth one step further away from the throne.

Henry was, in fact, prematurely old. The ulcerated sore in his leg was a constant trouble – if it ceased to suppurate and seemed to heal over, he fell into a fever, and surgeons must be called in to open it with their lancets. And although it is all too easy to dismiss him as a bloody-minded tyrant, it is also necessary to remember the man he had been; young; a poet and musician. His emotional life had foundered on the rock of Katharine of Aragon's obstinacy.

What brought about the near collapse of this his last marriage, was religious dissension. Katharine Parr was definitely a Protestant, and encouraged Protestantism; Henry was still Catholic, an *English* Catholic. He was – and had been, ever since he appointed Cranmer to declare his marriage to Katharine of Aragon null and void – occupying, so far as religion went, a kind of half-way house. He hated with equal vehemence those who still adhered to the Pope and those of the Lutheran persuasion.

Also, this, his last marriage, was barren. And that that was not his fault he could prove. By neither of her former husbands had Katharine become pregnant. Henry was, in the last year of their marriage, the last year of his life, almost persuaded to send her to the Tower as a heretic.

But she survived; perhaps because she was such a good nurse; she was Queen of England but she was willing to apply, with her own hands, the poultices which that ulcerated leg needed, and to sit nursing the leg in her lap.

Henry died when he was fifty-six; Katharine was thirty-four; still comely, very rich, and on good terms with all the three pale children whom Henry had named his heirs; Edward; Mary; Elizabeth.

She married, with what everybody thought indecent haste, the man she would have married four years earlier had the King not intervened, and her subsequent history is strongly interwoven with that of Elizabeth's youth. Meanwhile Edward, very Protestant and Mary extremely Catholic, were to succeed one another.

A woman of spirit and a good nurse; Katharine Parr. A portrait of about 1545 attributed to William Scrots.

KATHARINE PARRE

Mary Tudor

Queen in her own right
born 1516, married 1554, died 1558

Edward VI succeeded to the throne when he was nine years old and died when he was fifteen. Nobody expected him to live long. The general term 'consumption' was applied to his state, but it did not conform to pattern. When he died he had no hair, no finger-nails.

Mary was thirty-seven when her very Protestant young brother died; and although her father's will had definitely stated that she must succeed him, she did not come to the throne easily. Nothing had ever been easy for Mary Tudor, or ever would be. As a young child – but old enough to notice – she had seen her first betrothal to the Emperor come to grief, because her father's action against her mother had put her legitimacy in doubt. She had seen her mother thrust aside; Anne Boleyn crowned and then *her* daughter similarly smeared with the word bastard. So far as she could, Mary had been kind to the little Elizabeth. And once Katharine of Aragon was dead and the old question once and forever resolved, Mary had taken her place in court ceremonial. But she knew what it was to be despised and rejected, and what it meant to be poor.

She has always suffered by comparison with Elizabeth, made to seem pious and plain and dull; one writer even deduces that because her mother was Spanish, Mary was necessarily dark and sallow. In fact Katharine of Aragon was very fair, and Henry VIII's hair was red-gold and their daughter's was golden red and when she was young, pretty. When circumstances permitted she could be gay, and loved nothing better than a gamble. Despite her usually penurious state she was wildly generous, and despite her nickname of Bloody Mary, noticeably humane in a merciless age.

The Protestants did not wish her to become Queen. Their reasons were mixed; some genuine religious convictions and an eye to property. When Henry VIII broke with the Pope he dissolved the religious houses and gave

The grief-stricken and ill face of Mary Tudor in 1555.
Painting by Gerlach Flicke.

their vast properties to his friends. Mary, known to be not only Catholic but Papist, would, they feared, take away these great gifts. So they set up the Queen of their choice, the tragic young Lady Jane Grey, the grand-daughter of Henry's sister Mary. Her father-in-law, Duke of Northumberland, rather fancied himself as the power behind the throne of a puppet Queen.

Mary was in Kenninghall, in Norfolk, when she heard that her succession was being challenged. She acted with courage and promptitude. Kenninghall was not a place which could be defended, but in Suffolk there was a strongly fortified castle, well able to withstand a siege. With only a handful of followers and friends, Mary went to Framlingham and waited.

Within nine days the people of England had declared themselves; they wanted Mary. She rode to London and was well-received. Elizabeth went with her, a fact which proves that although Mary delighted in rich clothes and jewels, she was not fundamentally a vain woman, for she must have been aware of the contrast between her looks, faded by thirty-seven years, by grief and ill-health, and the brilliance of Elizabeth, twenty years old.

Queen for nine days; Lady Jane Grey.
A portrait by Master John.

She had always been kind to Elizabeth and continued to be so, walking about hand-in-hand with her, and always, when she dined in public, having her at her table.

Many people – Mary's father among them – would have cried, 'Off with their heads' and sent all the conspirators to the block. Mary was more moderate; the over-ambitious Duke of Northumberland was beheaded, Lady Jane Grey and her young husband went to the Tower, but were well-housed and allowed to walk about in the gardens. It was not until another rebellion was mounted with a view to putting Jane on the throne that Mary could be persuaded that while Jane lived she would never be safe on the throne. She signed the death-warrant with great reluctance.

Mary needed a settled, united England because she was anxious to get married, and bear a child as soon as possible. One of her advisers had told her, frankly, if unkindly, that she would be unwise to marry, since her prospects of motherhood were slight. But Mary desperately wanted an heir who would keep England Catholic. Elizabeth was behaving very well, attending Mass in the old style, but Mary knew that the Protestants in England regarded Elizabeth as their hope. She probably knew what an expert dissembler Elizabeth was.

Mary's reign, and what remained of her life, would have been happier could she have married Reginald Pole, a relative of hers who would not accept Henry as Head of the Church, had gone to the Continent, taken orders and become a Cardinal. In the circumstances the Pope would have released him from his vows, but neither Mary nor Cardinal Pole would have welcomed such a compromise. So she chose as her husband, Philip of Spain, who was the son of the Emperor Charles to whom, as a child, she had once been betrothed.

Nothing could have more displeased the English people. Philip already ruled so much of Europe, and all the New World; what would England, their England, mean to him? It would become just an appendage. Moreover Spain had become the headquarters of the Inquisition, an organisation devoted to the persecution of heretics. Every Protestant, secret or declared, was against this marriage, and so were many Catholics; being a Catholic did not necessarily make an Englishman pro-Spanish. The same people who had cheered Mary on her way to her coronation, stood in the same streets and flung filth at Philip and his attendants. Philip's dislike of England, his wish to do his duty and get away as soon as possible were understandable.

Of this marriage which made the Queen who had been so popular so unpopular, there was no child. Was this sterility a sign of God's wrath because she had not persecuted heretics severely enough? She started what are called the Marian persecutions. In fact they were mild enough; only about three hundred people in the famous fires at Smithfield. One victim was Cranmer who had been Henry's tool, and vacillated almost to the end; he recanted, and recanted on his recantation.

Philip made a first, prolonged visit to England; long enough if he were any judge to beget a child – he had been married before and knew about such matters. Then he went away to attend to other things and came back on a brief visit, just long enough to persuade Mary to bring England into his war against France and that resulted in the loss of Calais, all that was left of what England had once owned on the Continent. Little by little the vast provinces which Henry II and Eleanor of Aquitaine had inherited, and the later Plantagenets had fought for, had been nibbled away and there remained only Calais, a mere foothold on the Continent but important as a centre of trade. Now, because of this tangling of England with Spain, that too was lost, and Mary, who was, after all, half English, said that when she died the word Calais would be seen to be written on her heart.

But nothing else would matter much if only she could become pregnant and for a time she believed that she was. She increased in girth. She had also probably reached the menopause early.

Dropsy? It had afflicted her mother, dying in Kimbolton Castle. Or a tumour? One of those loathsome growths, parasites which kill the host on which they feed? Whatever it was it was not the child she longed for.

Like so many monarchs, Mary Tudor died lonely. The rising, not the setting, star was the focus of attention. The way people went rushing to Hatfield, where Elizabeth was at the time, taught that shrewd girl a lesson.

Mary had expressed a wish to be buried by her mother who lay, 'under the arms of Spain', in Peterborough Cathedral, but even in that she was frustrated and was given a pompous funeral at Westminster.

Elizabeth was there; perhaps remembering Mary's many kindnesses in the past when they were both regarded as bastards; perhaps musing upon Mary's mistakes.

Elizabeth Tudor

Queen in her own right
born 1533, died 1603

The most written-about Queen of England, possibly the most written-about woman in history; her relative and rival Mary Queen of Scots runs her close in the matter of mere wordage, but Mary Stuart's story is so consistent and comparatively understandable and almost everything about Elizabeth is mysterious and contradictory. She exercised such a spell over her own and succeeding generations that when in 1952 another Queen bearing her name came to the throne, many otherwise sensible and sober people talked about another Elizabethan Age.

Elizabeth was twenty-five when she became Queen, and those twenty-five years had been packed with incidents, vicissitudes and everything that makes for experience. Both Edward VI and Mary, while fond of her as a person, distrusted her politically as a likely centre of plots. She had spent some time as a prisoner – she scratched on a window pane with a diamond, 'Much suspected by me; nothing proved can be'. It sums up much of her life.

She had been involved in a scandal while still in her early teens. Katharine Parr married her handsome young lover and in proper step-maternal fashion took Elizabeth into her household where Thomas Seymour was soon paying Elizabeth more attention than was seemly. Edward VI's inquiries into what went on there brought up the answer – boisterous romping; but even to Tudor unprudish taste such romping seemed a little extreme. Much suspected; nothing proved.

Mary had so far restored Catholicism that there was only one bishop willing to officiate at Elizabeth's coronation; to all people of Catholic leanings – and some others – she was a bastard, born while Henry VIII was still the husband of Katharine of Aragon. But she had an ally, secret of course, of whom few books make mention. This was a curious man, an astrologer,

Elizabeth dancing at Court with Lord Leicester. Artist unknown.

a scholar and a wizard known as Doctor Dee. He consulted the stars and forecast for her a glorious and prosperous reign *provided* that she chose 15 January for her coronation. She took heed and was crowned on that day, a Sunday. On the previous day she had been carried, on an ornate litter, through the streets of London and that progress showed her, once and for all, that she had inherited her father's most enviable gift – that of being able to move crowds simply by appearing. In his day Henry had done many things of which most people disapproved but his personal popularity had survived. The mobs had howled in the streets, 'We want no Nan Bullen!' but nobody had added the seemingly inevitable corollary – 'We want no Henry'. Henry had had the capacity to do unpopular things without losing his popularity. Neither Edward nor Mary had inherited this almost mystic quality; Elizabeth did.

She did not say to the crowds that she would be good. She said, 'I will stand your good Queen', and old men turned away and wept because they were so much reminded of Henry VIII.

Elizabeth was always ready to refer to her father. In stormy Council meetings she would use oaths, telling men who made protests or offered unwelcome advice that they would not have dared to speak thus to her father. Once she made quite coarse reference to her sex. 'Had I been born crested, not cloven, you would not speak thus to me.'

Her mother she never mentioned; that shamed woman who had gone to the block, accused of adultery, incest and witchcraft, was best forgotten. But in her devious way Elizabeth was kind to all her mother's relatives, even to the relatives of Anne's step-mother, the homely little Norfolk woman, through whom by association, not blood, the Queen of England was in some way related to many farmers and shopkeepers.

The country to which she said she would stand as a good Queen was not in an enviable state when Elizabeth was crowned. On the Continent England had no friend, and Scotland was a declared enemy. All the Catholic world thought that Mary Queen of Scots' claim to the English throne was more valid than Elizabeth's. And England was relatively poor. France which now included all the lands once held by English Kings – even Calais – was much larger, much more populous: Spain, with her hold on the New World, was rich and powerful; even Portugal, a small country, was becoming rich through trading posts in Africa and in India.

Yet the little self-contained kingdom that was England was still desirable as an appendage; and for some years Elizabeth was desirable for herself. She had in all ten serious offers of marriage – one from Mary's husband, Philip of Spain.

How she countered these approaches, never saying 'Yes' or 'No', being civil, being deceptive, being in the end ridiculous, would make a big book.

Did she know that she could never bear a living child? Was, as somebody unkindly said, her body as crooked as her mind? Was she, as some people guess, not ruled by the cycles of the moon? We can never know. What we do know is that when she died and her private papers were sorted, there was a letter from Robert Dudley, Earl of Leicester, and on it written in Elizabeth's own unmistakable hand, three words. 'His last letter.'

Perhaps that tells all.

Rumour had of course been busy with the names of Elizabeth Tudor and Robert Dudley for many years. Mary Queen of Scots was able to say that she understood that the Queen of England was proposing to marry her Master of Horse – that was Dudley's position at the time; and he was lucky to have any position at all, for he was the son of that Duke of Northumberland who had tried to make Jane Grey Queen, and been beheaded. But Dudley was handsome and tall – of men Elizabeth often used the word 'little' in a derogatory sense; he was a year younger than Elizabeth, but already an expert in the art of pleasing without fawning. She loaded him with honours and lucrative appointments. Her fondness for him is shown by the failure of her usually sound judgment where he was concerned; more than once she entrusted him with military commands beyond his capacity. His personal courage was never in doubt, but he was not a strategist, and far too arrogant to be a good leader of men.

Would she have married him, had circumstances been different?

He had married, at the age of eighteen, a well endowed young woman, a knight's daughter, Amy Robsart. His own fortunes were at low ebb then, and when they took a turn for the better, his wife did not rise with him. She was never brought to Court and two years after Elizabeth's accession, she was found dead, in very mysterious circumstances indeed. Cumnor Place in Berkshire was a remote, semi-derelict place, once a religious house, and it belonged to one of Dudley's servants. Amy was Lady Dudley, and women of far lower rank were seldom left completely without attendants; she was, on a Sunday afternoon, and was found in the evening, dead at the foot of a flight of stairs. Her neck was broken, but her head-dress was in place and her clothing was not disarrayed.

There was an immediate scandal. People said that Amy Robsart had been murdered and that Elizabeth was aware of the plot. The Spanish Ambassador went so far as to say that the Queen had mentioned the death of Lady Dudley *on the day before it happened.*

Such talk in a country far less divided than England was at the time, would have spelt ruin for any other Queen. What protected Elizabeth? Doctor Dee's sorcery? Her own sensible behaviour? She ordered Dudley to leave Court, to go to his London house and stay there until an inquest had decided the cause of his wife's death. The jury decided that it was accidental. Dudley had never been near Cumnor; and if he had hired a murderer, the man was never named.

But the removal of the obstacle to the marriage between Robert Dudley and the Queen had raised an even more impassable barrier. They could never marry now; and perhaps in her heart, Elizabeth did not want marriage which for a woman always meant a certain amount of subjection.

Where religion was concerned, Elizabeth tried hard to put England back on the middle path which her father had thought possible. She was neither Catholic nor Protestant – some people said she had no religion. She disliked married clergy and was rude, in a polite way, to their wives; she equally disliked the sermons which were part of the Protestant morning ritual.

Hers was the time of the great seamen, Drake, Hawkins and Raleigh, all men who combined the role of explorer with that of pirate. She would tell them *not* to offend the Spanish, but she would buy shares in their ventures, whatever they might be, and take her percentage of the loot, well aware of its origin.

Elizabeth knew that Mary Queen of Scots claimed to be Queen of England, too; yet she sent her gifts and pleasant messages and finally a pretty young man, with Tudor blood, as a husband. Mary mismanaged things or was dead unlucky – most Stuarts were – and the Queen of Scots was obliged to take refuge in England. Elizabeth never received her; on the other hand she did not have her killed, as so many of her Council advised. It took her twenty years to agree that Mary of Scots was a danger to be exterminated.

As a child and a young girl she had been ill-provided for and had lacked even necessary clothes; so as Queen of England, no amount of finery could compensate for that early deprivation; she had a thousand dresses, so bejewelled and embroidered that they could stand alone; she had so many jewels that even in candlelight, the glitter of them was blinding to the eye. Yet in 1588 when her haphazard, rather amateur fleet went out to face the great Spanish Armada they were short of food and of ammunition.

'God blew with his winds and they were scattered', as the commemorative medal read. Certainly the Spanish Armada had been dogged by ill luck from the first. (It is a trivial thing, but earlier, when the Armada was being carefully prepared, Drake made a lightning attack on Cadiz and destroyed, amongst other things a lot of the seasoned wood which made the barrels upon which any fleet depended for water, for salt meat. And then Philip, usually so slow and cautious that he was called leaden-footed, for once in his life was hasty so that his great Armada set out with water leaking from the casks and meat going green.)

Elizabeth and all England, even the Catholics whom Philip counted on as allies, went into action, prepared to defend England; and Elizabeth went down to Tilbury where her land forces were gathered and made the best fighting speech of all time. Yet the makeshift army which she addressed in such stirring terms was under the command of her favourite who had twice before shown his inadequacy as a military leader.

However, some ninety-odd small ships, ill-provided, but with the wind in their favour, defeated one hundred and thirty. And whether Doctor Dee had a hand in it – one ability credited to sorcerers is to raise a wind – must be idle speculation.

Many writers – some of them poets – tend to regard Elizabeth's end as a judgment on her. One wonders why; she never did a deliberately cruel thing. The Poor Law Acts passed in her time were the first ever to make provision for those who were indigent through no fault of their own. With all her shifts and contradictions she had kept her word to stand as a good Queen, and she left England far stronger than she had found it.

Part of the nonsense about her is sentimental, pious or Puritan. Like any woman, once pretty, she tried to fight off old age; when her hair, which had been her great beauty, faded and fell, she took to a wig, and when her face wrinkled and collapsed she used cosmetics so freely that towards the end she looked more like the figurehead of a ship than a living woman. And even when she was seventy, she did not want to die. Who does?

She fought death as she fought life. She would not go to bed. One of her most faithful servants urged her to do so, 'Madam, you must go to bed'. He had one of the usual tart retorts. Little man, who was he to dictate to the Queen of England?

Remembering how people had left Mary's death-bed to hurry to Hat-

The 'Armada portrait' of Elizabeth I
by George Gower.

field and proclaim her as heir, she refused to nominate her successor and, finally, forced to it she gave the answer in the form of a question – Who but a King was fit to succeed a Queen? And that meant James of Scotland.

But in her down-going days, Elizabeth had said another memorable thing; she had told her faithful Lords and Commons that she prided herself on having ruled them by means of their love.

It was to be a long time, an unfortunately long time, before any King or Queen of England could make such a confident and such a true statement.

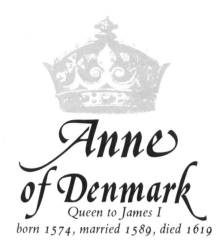

Anne
of Denmark
Queen to James I
born 1574, married 1589, died 1619

Anne deserves to be remembered if only for the fact that she was the only person to spark off one flash of courage in an otherwise cowardly man. James VI of Scotland and I of England was so timid that he is said to have flinched at the sight of an unsheathed sword, and he always had his clothes padded thickly for fear somebody might attempt to stab him; yet he set off, in a tiny not very seaworthy ship to fetch his bride from Norway, where she had been stranded by very bad weather. This was all the more creditable since the phenomenal winds were said to have been raised by witchcraft – and James believed in it.

She was pretty and sixteen years old; he was twenty-three and a very poor physical specimen indeed. He had been unable to walk until he was five years of age; by a curious coincidence, Anne had not been *allowed* to walk until she was nine; it was in tribute to her rank that she should be carried everywhere; once on her feet she walked very well, which James did not, and he was even more ungainly on a horse.

Part of Anne's dower were the islands of Shetland and Orkney. They were not in themselves of much value, but Scotland and Denmark both claimed them for purposes of strategy and prestige. (Now, in the twentieth century, both groups of islands are closely connected with the discovery of oil under the North Sea.) In return James settled upon his wife the palaces of Dunfermline and Falkland, with the estates that went with them.

They were married in Norway and then spent some time in Europe, visiting Anne's family and staying to see her sister married. Anne's coronation, at the palace of Holyroodhouse, did not take place until the next year; and it posed two extraordinary problems. James wanted to give his Queen a grand coronation – but he was so poor that he was obliged to borrow a pair of silk stockings for his own wear; and after what fashion should the ceremony be performed? The religious situation in Scotland was extremely confused. Part of the country, mainly the Highlands, were still Catholic; there were ordinary Protestants who did not accept the authority of the Pope, but did acknowledge bishops, and extreme Protestants who disliked any such appointments. By begging for gifts and demanding loans, James was able to give Anne a splendid ceremony, the religious part of it being performed by a minister, not a bishop. There was one of those sermons which Elizabeth of England so much detested; and then James himself placed the crown on Anne's head and put the sceptre into her hand.

Their first child, Prince Henry was born in 1594 and was almost immediately sent to Stirling Castle to be reared by the Earl and Countess of Mar. Anne did not take kindly, or bow meekly, to this decision; she wanted to keep her child with her; but James explained that it was the custom of the country and she was forced to give way. Two years later she gave birth to a girl, Elizabeth, destined to become Queen of Bohemia for a brief time, but destined also to give the Hanoverians their claim to the English throne a hundred and eighteen years later. The young Princess was likewise consigned to the care of a nobleman. Anne had another child, a girl who died young, and then in 1600, the boy who was to become Charles I of England.

The regular appearance of babies is no proof of a happy marriage and there are indications that Anne gave James cause for jealousy, not in the crude physical sense, but by openly admiring and favouring younger and more handsome men. She was gay in a remarkably dour Court. There is something pathetic in James's remark when she said that some young lord was the handsomest man she knew. 'You might have excepted me', he said.

The great Queen of England was in failing health. Towards James her attitude had varied over the years and she had never expressed a wish that he should succeed her. She died and men on swift horses set off for Scotland. James was not unprepared, he had his spies and his friends in England.

Anne, expecting another child, did not accompany James. The baby was born and soon died; Anne, perhaps not yet quite recovered, and with no husband to control her, had a virulent quarrel with the Earl and Countess of Mar, and then, still in a bad temper, set out for England. There she refused to accept as her ladies-in-waiting those who by rank were entitled to such posts; she preferred those she had brought from Scotland. One lady retaliated by saying that even a brief visit to the Queen had afflicted her with lice.

It was a pity that the first coronation of a King and Queen of England and Scotland should *not* have been a glorious affair; but the pestilence was stalking the streets. It always was, in summer, and it was now July. There comes down to us a record of pestilences of exceptional severity; the Black Death; the Great Plague of London, but wherever people lived together in any number, with no sanitation and tainted sources of drinking water, the plague in this form or that was a constant threat. It was bad enough in the

*Anne of Denmark with the dogs she loved so well. Painting by
Paul van Somer.*

summer of 1603 to make this exceptional coronation almost a private
ceremony.

If Anne of Denmark is shown to posterity as a rather irritable and irritat-
ing woman, she may perhaps be excused, for she was one of those unfortunate women married to a bi-sexual man. Admittedly, when James wrote

to her he began the letter with, 'My Heart' and ended it, 'Your James', but his male favourites were notorious. Still, she had her children and she would snatch any bit of gaiety when she could.

Then, in 1612, her elder son, Henry, Prince of Wales – brilliantly clever, and very well-grown, six feet tall when he was seventeen, a son of whom any woman could be proud – began to dwindle and sicken. There were the usual excuses; he had over-exerted himself in the tiltyard; he had gone swimming, late in the evening, after a full supper, in the Thames. What ailed him was probably tuberculosis, a disease then not understood and one for which there was no cure.

Except, perhaps . . .

Confined in the Tower at the time was Sir Walter Raleigh, one of Queen Elizabeth's favourites, one of her buccaneers. James had imprisoned him to please the King of Spain, but the Prince of Wales had visited him and become, in a fashion, his friend.

Raleigh had been explorer as well as pirate in the New World, and his lively, insatiable mind had made him look into the cures which the primitive native people relied upon. Particularly a fever cure, called quinine. In his usual flamboyant way, he boasted that this would cure all diseases, except those caused by poison. The Queen now appealed to him and he supplied some of his wonderful panacea, despite which Prince Henry died. His mother, beside herself with grief, said that her son had been poisoned by the King's current favourite, and therefore, by inference, by the King himself. There she did James an injustice; whatever his faults, he was a good father. Despite his mortal dread of infection he had remained by his son's bedside until the end, as the Queen had not.

The accusation caused some scandal which soon blew over and James bore her no resentment. It is noticeable however that the parents did not hasten towards one another in their mutual grief, though they were, later, together at the marriage of their daughter.

Soon after that Queen Anne's health began to fail. She went to Bath, and thinking the cure beneficial, made a long stay there. Since she suffered from a cough and haemorrhages of the lungs it seems likely that she was suffering from the same disease as that which had killed her son. On her it worked more slowly and she lived, but in poor health, until she was forty-six. The King, on a journey, was ill himself at the time in Hertfordshire and the person closest to her when she died was one of the women she had brought with her from Denmark.

James appeared to be deeply grieved by her death, and it is possible that despite their quarrels, she had exercised some influence upon him. He outlived her by seven years and his devotion to male favourites became more conspicuous. Manners at Court declined to a point at which no lady wished to be seen there.

Henrietta Maria

Queen to Charles I
born 1609, married 1625, died 1669

If Anne of Denmark had slightly influenced James I, her successor, Henrietta of France, exercised almost complete control over Anne's son, Charles I.

Henrietta Maria's father was that Henry IV of France who is remembered for two statements. He had been born and bred as a Protestant, but when all other heirs to the throne of France were dead and he was offered it on condition that he became Catholic, he is reputed to have said, 'Paris is worth a Mass'. When he was King of France, he said that it was his wish to make the country so prosperous that every peasant should have a chicken in the pot every Sunday.

Though he was handsome and had beautiful manners, it had not been easy to find a bride for Charles, who on his brother's death became Prince of Wales.

James I's original choice, a princess of Spain, was not successful because when he sent Charles to Spain to woo the lady, he sent with him the latest and greatest favourite, George Villiers, Duke of Buckingham whose arrogant, outrageous behaviour so incensed the King of Spain that all negotiations were broken off. Bargaining for the Spanish marriage, James had sacrificed Sir Walter Raleigh, agreed to lift the penal laws against Catholics in England, and allow the Princess freedom to worship in her own way and to bring up her children in her own faith.

But that match came to nothing, and with much the same concessions – except that Sir Walter Raleigh could not be beheaded a second time – France was approached.

Henrietta Maria was a third daughter and therefore fairly expendable; but of a family of beauties she was considered to be the most beautiful. Charles fell in love with her.

At first, coming to a country whose religion was different from her own,

*Henrietta Maria with the husband whose coronation and
execution she did not share. Painting by Van Dyck.*

she was tactful. Asked if she could receive a Huguenot – the Huguenots were
French Protestants who had fled to England – she said, 'Why not? My father
was one'. So he had been, until he thought Paris a fair exchange for a Mass.

She was not always so tactful.

She refused to be crowned in a Protestant ceremony; refused even to be
present, 'behind a lattice', in Westminster Abbey, while her husband was
crowned. Instead, surrounded by her French ladies and attendants, she stood
at a window in Whitehall and watched the procession. What could be more
offensive to the English people?

Charles had many bad advisers, but the worst was the wife whom he
adored. She came from France where such a thing as a Parliament was
unknown, and whenever Charles fell out with his Parliament, Henrietta
Maria would urge him to rule like a King of France.

She did not invariably get her own way; Charles, though infatuated with
her, had more knowledge of the country over which he ruled; he sent most
of her retinue back to France, and when their first child was born, insisted
upon a Protestant baptism. But that boy was born prematurely and soon
died. Just on one year later she had a second son, the good lusty boy whom

all royal families longed for, but even successful motherhood did not endear her to the people. This baby, one day to be Charles II, and Henrietta Maria's next child, one day to become James II, were both baptized in Church of England fashion; so were her daughters.

(All this religious dissension makes tedious reading, but people then thought it important and even now the rule holds; the throne of England must not be occupied by a professing Roman Catholic.)

Encouraged by his wife, Charles argued with, tried to defy, his various Parliaments and civil war resulted.

Henrietta Maria was not watching from that window at Whitehall when Charles, with dignity, went to his death. Quite early in the war she had gone to ask help of the French; but they had their own troubles just then.

After the Civil War in England was over, Henrietta Maria, once her father's pet, and then her husband's darling, faced bleak poverty. She was reduced to the state where she was obliged to appeal to Oliver Cromwell, Lord Protector of England, to send her the revenue which as a King's widow was her right. Then her refusal to be crowned bounced back on her. Cromwell could say, with some truth, that she had never been crowned Queen of England and therefore had no rights at all.

She survived poverty and humiliation and had enough spirit left in 1660, when Charles II was restored to the throne, without a blow being struck, to scold him for appearing to be, pretending to be, a good Church of England man. She scolded her second son, the Duke of York even more harshly – he had married a commoner, far below him in rank, Anne Hyde.

She came back to England just after Charles' restoration, when the rebound from the Puritan Commonwealth was at its height. She was given a great welcome. But she was as arbitrary as ever; she could not bear to occupy any apartment which she had ever shared with her dead husband; she could not bear the sight of Whitehall where he had been beheaded. At a time when Charles II, one of the kindest of men, was ready to cast off the past and rejoice, there was his mother, shedding tears, wringing her hands, calling herself the Unhappy Queen.

Everybody about the new Court hoped that the Queen Mother would soon go back to France. She did so, but only for a short time. She was back in England in 1662 to take part in all the celebrations which attended Charles' marriage to Catherine of Braganza – a match of which Henrietta fully approved. She was again well-received, installed in Somerset House, granted an income that not only covered her expenses but allowed her to be very charitable. But England was not her country, and she went back to France to die. Resilient to the end, she refused until a few hours before her death to take the opium pills which her physician prescribed for the relief of pain. She died in 1669, having reached, despite all vicissitudes, the age of sixty.

Catherine of Braganza

Queen to Charles II
born 1638, married 1660, died 1705

Catherine was a princess of Portugal and it is surprising that she should be the first of her race to be Queen of England, for the Portuguese were England's oldest friends, and the steadiest. The Portuguese never forgot how a company of English knights, on their way to a Crusade in the Holy Land, halted at Portugal for supplies. The Portuguese King asked them why they must go so far to fight the Infidel, his country had been over-run by the Moors; why not strike at them? The Crusaders did so, and so effectually that Portugal was freed of Moors centuries before her sister country, Spain.

Catherine brought with her a very rich dowry, for Portugal had in the previous century and a half emerged as a colonial power. Three hundred and fifty thousand pounds was more than any Queen of England had brought to her husband, and there were territorial gifts as well; Tangier in Africa, Bombay in India. She was Catholic and the marriage treaty gave her the right to exercise her own religion.

Charles was thirty when he married, Catherine was twenty-two, but their past experiences were unimaginably different. He had fought in the Civil War, escaped with his life and nothing else, lived through eleven years of exile, moving about, glad of any hospitality, however meagre and grudging, getting a worm's eye view of the world and of his fellow-men. Catherine had lived in almost nun–like seclusion, and when her betrothal to Charles finally set her free of the hampering rules surrounding the conduct of a princess of Portugal, her first act was to make a series of pious pilgrimages. Charles was the wittiest, most sophisticated man of his time; one of his mistresses had already borne his child – the ill-fated Duke of Monmouth; Catherine was utterly naïve – but anxious to please.

Descriptions of her vary. One gathers that she looked better in the easy, rather romantic English clothes then in fashion, than in the stiff out-dated

A miniature of Catherine of Braganza painted by Samuel Cooper.

Portuguese style; most eye-witnesses mention that her teeth protruded – not necessarily a disadvantage. But had she been of angelic beauty it is unlikely that she would have held Charles II to strict marital fidelity for long. He liked women, and he liked change. But he was always kind to her; once when she suffered the humiliation of being sick in his presence, he held the bowl and steadied her and did the necessary cleaning up afterwards. That his marriage and Catherine's arrival in England should coincide with his complete infatuation with a mannerless, insensitive, arrogant woman – Lady Castlemaine – was an unfortunate trick of Fate.

In the long cavalcade of Queens, Catherine of Braganza does not stand out as a conspicuous figure but she must have been a woman with exceptional self-control. No child of her own, yet she was kind to Charles' bastards and to the other children about the Court.

Catherine lived through the Great Plague of London, the last of the full-scale epidemics, when in one week of a glorious hot June, ten thousand people died in London. She lived through the Great Fire of London when her husband and his brother showed themselves to be courageous, and kindly, helping to extinguish the flames and helping to find homes for the homeless. She lived through a determined attempt on the part of the anti-Catholic group to prove that her marriage to Charles could be ignored because he had formerly been legally married to Lucy Walters, his mistress, the mother of the Duke of Monmouth. Put into the perspective of history such a suggestion may sound trivial, but set in human terms, it reads differently, a final affront to a woman who had been very patient, much neglected and almost infinitely obliging. Nothing came of this attempt to push her aside; Charles was against it. So Catherine of Braganza did not suffer the long torment of Katharine of Aragon. She was still Queen when Charles died.

He died as he had lived, witty, cynical, gay. He suffered his fatal stroke on a Monday morning and did not die until Friday. He apologised to his attendants for being so long a-dying.

During those days Catherine came and went. In one conscious moment Charles begged her to forgive him for the wrongs he had done her, and she was so overcome by emotion that she swooned and had to be carried away.

After Charles' death she did not, as she could have done, and as might have been expected, leave England and return to her native Portugal. She stayed on in England for seven years, leading much the same kind of life as she had led as Queen Consort. James II, Charles' brother, was friendly and kind; she was past the age where anything exciting was likely to happen to her; she was, in fact, complaisant, but not yet entirely removed from the hurly-burly of life.

The Duke of Monmouth, Charles' first and most dearly loved illegitimate son, was persuaded to make a bid for the throne; Protestant against Catholic. The rebellion failed; hundreds of simple peasants who had supported Monmouth were condemned to death by Judge Jeffries, in what was called the Bloody Assize. Monmouth was condemned, too, and Catherine, possibly remembering the handsome little boy, the engaging young man whom she had accepted and whom Charles had loved, made a bold petition for his life. It was rejected. James was not hostile to the sister-in-law whose lack of children had led him to becoming King, but he could not afford to spare the handsome, popular young Protestant about whom further plots were certain to centre.

James II did not reign long, and when he was compelled to flee from England, leaving the throne to his daughter, Mary and her husband, William of Orange, Catherine's position became very difficult. The 'Glorious Revolution', which had dethroned James had been an entirely Protestant one; Mary and William were both earnest Protestants and Mary was definitely unfriendly to her aunt. Catherine, because of her marriage treaty, was protected from the ordinary persecution which Catholics had to endure, but she suffered in minor ways. Mary did not want her in London, she must confine herself to the country. The number of Catholics she could have in her household was limited. Finally she decided to return to Portugal.

She had always received a substantial income and in the seven years of her widowhood had lived modestly, so she was able to make generous provision for all her English servants who remembered her kindly all their lives.

In Portugal she was given a royal welcome, both by her brother, the King, and by ordinary people. She and her sister-in-law developed a particularly close friendship. So her last years, when she became Queen Regent of Portugal, were happy. There are occasional references to failing health, but she lived to be sixty-seven. When she died she was given a funeral suitable to her rank as a princess of Portugal and a Queen of England.

Mary
of Modena

Queen to James II
born 1658, married 1673, died 1718

James' first wife, Anne Hyde, whom many people regarded as quite unsuitable as a choice, died after a reasonably happy marriage. James, like his brother, was kind if not always faithful. Anne had several children, of whom only the two daughters, Mary and Anne survived.

Left to himself James would probably have married another Englishwoman of good, if not royal, family; but he was now near the throne, since Charles had no legitimate offspring; so a more suitable match must be made. Charles II spoke with less than his usual courtesy when he told his brother that he was now too old to make a fool of himself for a second time.

Various ladies were inspected. There was a tacit agreement that to placate James for being forced into an arranged marriage, his new bride should be attractive. Mary of Modena was said to be beautiful – and all the pictures of her substantiate this claim; she also had the advantage of being very young; only fifteen. Modena did not offer much in the way of political allegiance; it was merely an Italian Duchy, its Duke dead, his heir a minor and everything in the hands of his mother, who sounds a detestable character. She forced such a strict régime of study upon her son that his doctors warned of ruined health. She replied that she would rather have no son than one who was a nit-wit.

One would have thought that Mary would have welcomed any marriage, for the Duchess was equally severe with her; but Mary, though exceptionally well-educated in some ways, did not know where England was, had never heard of the Duke of York, and when told that he was forty years old, burst into tears and said she would sooner be a nun. Her mother was not the woman to heed such protests. Mary of Modena was married by proxy – in a Catholic ceremony – and then journeyed overland to Calais, crossed the Channel and came to the country of whose existence she had until lately been quite unaware.

Mary of Modena, the mother of the 'Old Pretender',
by Simon Verelst.

James was enchanted by her. They had a second marriage, this time a Protestant ceremony.

She then became part of a luxurious and licentious Court, towards which she did her innocent best to adjust; joining in the card games of which she had no knowledge, being civil to the King's mistresses. She became fond enough of James to grieve over his infidelities. Catherine of Braganza was kind to her, and she in turn was kind to her step-daughters, Mary and Anne.

She had two daughters, one died in infancy, the other lived to be five; she had a son who died soon after birth. There was still no male heir to the English throne when Charles II died and James and Mary were crowned in a gorgeous ceremony, Protestant in ritual, though James was known for his Catholic adherence and Mary's Catholicism had been accepted from the first.

It is possible that if Mary, now Queen of England, had not had another child – and that child a boy – the Glorious Revolution, as it was called, might never have happened. James was getting old – fifty-two when he came to the throne; his daughter Mary, a Protestant, married to the Protestant Prince of Orange was his heir presumptive and if their marriage proved to be unproductive, there was Anne, married to George of Denmark and already started on her tragic motherhood road. Most English people of all persuasions were prepared to wait. But in June 1688 Mary of Modena gave birth to another child, a boy.

There is a ridiculous story concerning his birth. It was said that the Queen was not actually pregnant, merely pretending to be so, and that the baby was smuggled into her bed in a warming-pan. The Princess Anne was not entirely guiltless concerning this story – she said that the Queen had already been careful to retire to another room to dress and to undress. A hint that Mary's figure did not bear inspection. Yet the boy was born, and Catherine of Braganza was there at the birth.

This baby, doomed to be known all his life as the Old Pretender, had as clear a right to the English throne as any man ever had, but his birth brought the religious squabble to a head. His father was a crypto-Catholic, his mother an open one. What could be hoped of him?

The ordinary people, both of England and Scotland, were prepared to ignore the fact that this little boy was a threat to Protestantism; they simply seized on an excuse to make merry, with feasts and bonfires and church bells ringing, and firework displays. The King was in transports of delight – but not to the extent of heeding the Queen's sensible suggestion that such a joyful event might be marked by granting a general amnesty to all who were in prison for religious offences. He did however agree to found a home for orphaned children.

Meanwhile the doctors, from ignorance, not malice, were doing their best to kill the young Prince. He was hardly a day old before they administered a dose of some mysterious substance, 'said to be good for babies'. It did not agree with him; so they repeated the dose! Then one of them produced a wonderful theory; the Queen's other children had not flourished because they had been breast-fed; therefore there was something wrong with her milk. They took him from the breast and tried to feed him on water gruel – a mixture of barley flour, water, sugar and a few currants. On this horrifying diet he became very ill indeed and his life was only just saved by

*The birth of the 'Old Pretender'; no sign of a warming pan
in this medal.*

the hiring of a wet nurse. Properly suckled he flourished; and immediately the enemies of the royal family were saying that the wet nurse was his real mother, and that the baby was the son of a bricklayer.

It is not pleasant to associate the boy's two half-sisters with the spreading of rumours concerning his illegitimacy; but two facts stand out. His birth had been sudden and slightly premature. Anne who suffered just such a sudden and premature child-bearing did not stand up and say, 'The same thing happened to me'. And Mary who had always been on fond and friendly terms with Catherine of Braganza changed her attitude. *Why?* One can only surmise that it was because Catherine had been present at the birth and was willing to testify that Mary *had* borne this child in a perfectly normal way; without benefit of warming-pans.

James' elder daughter had married an intensely ambitious man, and since it now seemed unlikely that she would inherit the throne of England, he made an invasion, landing at Torbay. James, Mary and the infant were instantly deserted. James sent Mary and the young Prince to France, where they were kindly received by Louis XIV, and after some days, during which Mary suffered agonies of apprehension, James followed them.

The rest of her story has no place here; the French, and the English exiles were always scrupulous about giving James his rightful title, and the Queen hers; but they rang hollow. James died in 1701, Mary seventeen years later. She had lived to see the failure of the 1715 uprising in favour of the Stuart cause, the immediate result of which was more exiles, calling themselves Jacobites. The King of France had made her a generous allowance, and she had spent it all on helping the exiles.

She went to her grave as Queen of England; not one of the most famous, but in character one of the best.

Mary II

Queen in her own right and Queen to William III
born 1662, married 1677, died 1694

Everything about this brief reign is very contradictory. There was no precedent for it. Mary Tudor had married Philip of Spain – but he had never called himself King of England.

And while James Stuart, Mary's half-brother was alive, her claim to the throne was, to say the least, debatable.

She was born in 1662, just at the time when England was still intoxicated by the Restoration of her uncle Charles II and the lifting of the strict Puritan rule of Cromwell which had closed all theatres and alehouses and even forbidden the keeping of Christmas. She was one of those healthy children who could survive whatever the doctors decreed, and when she was two she had a sister, Anne, to be company for her. Mary was nine when her mother died, but she never lacked care and attention. But nine, in an age when maturity came earlier, was probably old enough for Mary to regard her own prospects quite seriously. If her aunt, Catherine of Braganza continued to be childless . . . and presently, if her step-mother, Mary of Modena failed to produce a son, then Mary was heir to the throne.

Her marriage was an arranged one and rather a curious choice. That part of Europe which we now know as Holland was then a loose confederation of independent states which had fought for many years to free themselves from Spain and having done so, felt the need for a focal point. William of Orange did not inherit Holland, he was elected. He was Protestant.

Mary was fifteen and he was almost twenty-seven when they married – the bride being given away by the King, Charles II. It would be difficult for the most ardent romanticist to catch a glimmer of glamour about the bride-groom. He was consumptive, and asthmatic, fluent in seven languages he never wasted a word, and his manners are said to have been repulsive. In what way exactly we are not told but he was sufficiently lacking in manners

In the immortal words of 1066 *and* All That *'WilliamandMary the Orange'. A miniature by Peter Hoadley.*

to show his displeasure during his marriage visit to England, because during it Mary of Modena bore a son – one of those who did not live long. Neither Charles' nor Mary's father would have allowed ill-temper to show in the circumstances, but William had a one-track mind; he wanted to break the power of France and to be King of England would be a great help towards this end.

Mary was neither very happy, nor very healthy during her eleven years in Holland; she found the climate damp and cold, and the solid Dutch burghers dull, though she learned to love them and their countryside in due course. Also, surprisingly, considering his solemnity, his taciturnity and his lack of physical attractions, William was an unfaithful husband. Two of the English ladies whom Mary had taken with her, the Villiers sisters, became his mistresses. Her hopes of motherhood were disappointed. Hers was a wasted youth.

Charles died and James succeeded him to the disgust of William who had expected the English to repudiate a Catholic King at once. And after he became King, James behaved towards his second daughter, Anne, in a manner which could only have caused some apprehension in Holland. Anne was granted the kind of allowance which usually only went to a presumptive heir; and Anne, married to the stupid but handsome George of Denmark, was proving to be remarkably fertile. (In all she had nineteen children, only one of whom survived infancy, a poor afflicted child.) With each of Anne's pregnancies both William and Mary must have felt that perhaps the English might prefer the princess who had remained in England and had a child, to the one who had lived in Holland and by her marriage become entangled in continental affairs. Anne's husband, though Danish by birth, was only a younger son, and it suited him well to remain in England, sharing his wife's splendid income and all the favours which her father showered upon her.

However, when James, 'the Old Pretender' was born, and despite everything, lived, and William took action, most people of importance flocked to him. He and Mary succeeded and reigned for five years – the period known as William-and-Mary – during which, under Dutch influence, some singularly fine houses and furniture came into being.

William and Mary were crowned together in a ceremony which again had its contradictory elements. A second orb must be provided for Mary, but she was crowned with the Queen Consort's Crown which James had had made for Mary of Modena. Much of the ritual which had embellished all the Kings of England – and two Queens, Mary and Elizabeth Tudor – was now centred about William. Yet to those who could ignore the rights of her father and her little half-brother, she was Queen, and William was here simply because he was her husband. When it came to offering the sword at the altar, they carried it between them; an awkward procedure, for she was tall and majestic; he was short and thin. James II had gone from England with the Coronation Ring on his finger; so two new ones had been made.

In his silent, subfusc way, William was jealous of his wife and the remaining five years of her life were little happier than her years in Holland. William missed no opportunity of making her feel a second-class citizen; he rebuked her in public, even for so small a thing as going to consult a fortune-teller. From overseas there came a constant flow of pamphlets and cruel cartoons all accusing her of having snatched the throne from her father; and she and her sister Anne bickered about trivial things – such as which of them should have the use of Hampton Court.

Mary derived some pleasure from gardens and since William decided to build a new palace at Kensington, she had scope for this hobby. The best bulbs in the world came, then as now, from Holland, and since Dutch and English ships were now everywhere in the known world, many plants hitherto unknown in England were introduced. Mary also sought solace,

The formal gardens at Kensington Palace looked like this
when they were first created by Mary.

as many frustrated people do, in the comforts of the table. In 1694 she became
ill; her physicians could not decide whether she was suffering from measles
or small-pox – and indeed in an adult a bad attack of measles can very much
resemble the more deadly complaint. For either a body too well-fed is small
advantage. She was only thirty-two and death did not come easily, almost
to the end she suffered delusions and raved about spies and Popish plots. She
died in 1694. Mary was buried, with all the ceremony due to a Queen, in
Westminster Abbey. Her death, though it caused no commotion, set hopes
soaring – in the group about her sister Anne and in the Jacobites overseas.
What now?

The answer, for eight years, was nothing. William III, despite all his dis-
advantages of physique and manner was a good soldier and most English
people preferred to allow things to go on as they were under his governance,
which had in fact enormously strengthened the rule of Parliament.

This queer double – and then single – reign brought enormous power to
the people of England. Before it all the revenue had been put into the monarch's pocket. If he chose to keep up an army or a navy, or squander the
money on personal pleasures, that had been his right. It was no longer so.
The Parliament in the reign of Mary and William took control, allowing
what it considered a suitable income to the royal family. The Parliament
called it the Civil List; it bears the name to this day.

Anne

Queen in her own right
born 1665, married 1683, died 1714

See colour plate facing page 160.

Anne had to wait until she was thirty-seven before she became Queen; any beauty she had ever possessed had vanished; like her sister she was fond of her food; her health was not good and repeated pregnancies had ruined her figure. There is something symbolic – and sad – about the fact that all that is interesting in her twelve years' reign centres about other people. The Duke of Marlborough won some famous victories and his wife, first as friend, then as enemy, of the Queen, draws all the attention.

Her husband, George of Denmark is also a negative character. Charles II summed him up when he came to England more or less on approval. He said he'd tried George drunk and he'd tried George sober and found nothing in him either way. Anne's husband certainly did his duty as a begetter of children, but if he had supplied her with what her weak, yielding nature needed, she would not have turned to women and allowed them to dominate her in such extraordinary fashion.

Anne was not even a good mother. One of her children lived past early infancy; he was abnormal, with a hydrocephalic head and weak legs. He had a poor sense of balance, and knew it, so he welcomed help on stairs. His father beat him for accepting help. Anne did nothing. And when the poor little boy did not cry when told that his aunt Mary was dead, Anne rebuked him. He was just five years old at the time! He died, perhaps fortunately, when he was eleven years old. It is nice to think that he had a happy birth-day, a mock review of his miniature troops, and it showed a faint glimmer of hope for medicine in the future that a doctor, called to his death-bed, asked had he been bled? Told that this was so, this unorthodox man, Doctor Radcliffe, said, 'Then you have destroyed him. I will not prescribe'.

Anne was weak and vacillating, and where her favourites were concerned, plain silly, but her reign is remembered, for its good building, furniture, silver-ware and for its literature. Pope and Steele and Addison were all productive during her reign.

She died so slowly and was rumoured to be dead so often before she ceased to breathe that for many years the words 'Queen Anne is dead' made a sick joke.

Her death left England in a curious position. Her half-brother James, still in his twenties, able and willing, and undoubtedly a Stuart, in looks and behaviour no bricklayer's son, was waiting. But he was a Catholic. So the people in power in England chose to offer the empty throne to George of Hanover who had some Stuart blood. His grandmother was that beautiful Elizabeth Stuart, daughter of James I who had briefly been Queen of Bohemia.

Whether George of Hanover even wanted to be King of England is doubtful; he was elderly, fifty-four years old; he spoke no English. And he brought England no Queen, so her story has no place here, which is rather a pity because hers is a romantic story – as romance is reckoned. Having given her tough, soldierly little husband two children, she took a lover. What happened to him is a matter of speculation, what happened to her is fact. She was imprisoned in one of her husband's castles, a place called Ahlden; allowed an airing every afternoon, always on the same road, four miles out, four miles back. She was probably a tough character, too, for she bore her punishment for thirty-two years. Her son became George II of England.

A scene on the Thames showing two barges bearing Queen Anne's cypher. Artist unknown.

Caroline of Ansbach

Queen to George II
born 1683, married 1705, died 1737

The Hanoverians were invited to occupy the English throne because of their strain of Stuart blood and because of their uncompromising Protestantism. George I when he first arrived in England in 1714 knew no English and at the age of fifty-four was unlikely to learn much. He was the first King to employ a Prime Minister – such an appointment was necessary when the monarch had no knowledge of the language or the customs or laws of his new country.

George II, son of the first George, was German born, and already thirty-one years old when he came to England, and he was married to Caroline of Ansbach, one of those small German principalities, similar to Hanover itself.

There is an unshiftable dullness about the early Hanoverians; they came from small, relatively poor countries, they had no style, no flamboyance; yet their manners were stiffly formal. So were their clothes. Their English – when they attempted it – was a matter of ridicule to their subjects, most of whom could speak nothing but English. They somehow contrived to make even their lecheries dull. Both George I and George II had mistresses – but none of them has come down to us a second Nell Gwynne. Queen Caroline is said to have retained some hold upon George II by choosing his mistresses, careful to see that they were uglier than herself, an indirect reflection upon her own looks.

That George II, despite his infidelities, did respect and trust his wife was proved by the fact that when he was abroad – he was always happier in Hanover than in England – he left her as Regent. Since William I left Matilda in such office it has always been a kind of test, not of how attractive a Queen was as a woman, but of her husband's estimation of her as a person.

*Caroline of Ansbach; trusted by her husband as Regent. A state portrait
from the studio of Jervas.*

There was an ill-intentioned rhyme going the rounds:
> You may strut, dapper George, but 'twill all be in vain,
> We know 'tis Queen Caroline, not you, that reign.

(In the interest of rhyme grammar must sometimes be sacrificed.)

Yet George II in himself was not negligible; he was honest, painstaking and indisputably brave. He was the last King of Britain to take his place on a battlefield. It was during the War of the Austrian Succession and English and Hanoverians were fighting the French. George's horse ran away with him, so he dismounted and put himself at the head of a troop saying that now he could be sure of standing his ground. It was a gesture which should have made him popular – especially as that battle was a victory.

One thing which the Hanoverians brought to England alongside the style of building which we call Georgian, and of which the Herrenhausen in Hanover was the begetter, was a resurgence of family dissension. Fathers and sons seemed bound to quarrel and to take opposite sides in any dispute. Queen Caroline may have ruled her husband very subtly and cleverly, but she could not make him love his first-born, Frederick, Prince of Wales. Did she love him, with all his faults? Mothers do tend to favour their sons, but if she had a leaning towards Frederick she concealed it so carefully that he disliked her too.

Frederick and his wife – another princess from that apparently inexhaustible supply in mid-Germany, Augusta of Saxe-Gotha – were actually with the King and Queen at Windsor when Augusta began to suffer the pains of labour. Frederick was so absolutely determined that his mother should have no hand in, not even be a witness to, this confinement that he hustled his wife into a carriage and drove at full speed to their London house. There they were not expected and nothing was ready. Even sheets were lacking and Augusta's bed was spread with tablecloths which were available. (This sounds absurd, but it was to be another hundred years before anyone seriously questioned the arrangements of royal households, the proliferation of appointments, the who-does-what which made for muddle, inefficiency and more discomfort than any private citizen would have tolerated.)

Caroline died before her husband, and perhaps because she realised how much he had depended upon her, murmured, on her death-bed, that he should marry again. Somebody once called him an honest blockhead, and he made an honest blockhead's reply. 'No', he said through his tears, 'No. I shall have mistresses'.

The curious tribute may have pleased her. She was leaving a vacancy behind her. Frederick, Prince of Wales was dead, so Augusta could never become Queen. Not until the little boy, born between the tablecloths and being reared, with his sisters, in strict seclusion at Kew House, chose himself a wife, would there be another Queen in England.

Charlotte
of Mecklenburg-Strelitz

Queen to George III
born 1744, married 1761, died 1818
See colour plate facing page 161.

It suited Augusta, the Dowager Princess of Wales to assume that George II's Court was an immoral place, quite unfit for her children to frequent; it gave her more control over their upbringing and education, matters on which she held strong views. Life at Kew House was family life, unpretentious, orderly and quiet. Whether or not it was the ideal upbringing for the boy who was to become King of England is open to question; a little more contact with people of varying opinions might have rendered George III slightly less inflexible.

And for all her care, Augusta could not change the Hanoverian characteristics. George, her son, became King when he was twenty-two; and long before that scandal had busied about him. He was said to have had a violent love affair with – of all people – a Quaker woman, Hannah Lightfoot. It was even said that he had made a secret marriage, begotten a child. Some authorities say that the child was a daughter, but there are other, more fascinating stories of a man, mysterious and unforthcoming, but rich, and with some of his silver plate bearing the royal arms, living in South Africa.

It was plain that George must be married as soon as possible. The Hannah Lightfoot affair had been shuffled under wraps and now he was expressing a wish to marry a pretty woman, Lady Sarah Lennox. Nothing against her except that she was not royal and to pick out one aristocratic English family for such advancement would certainly offend others. (Edward IV had done it; Henry VIII had done it – four times – but things had changed since their days.)

George III's bride was hand-picked; the sister of the ruling Duke of Mecklenburg-Strelitz, Protestant, and young, a potential child-bearer. She was young, eighteen, but even records – inclined to be sycophantic – describe her as plain; short and spare of figure, with a nose too flat and a

Study for a sketch of Charlotte by Benjamin West.

mouth too large. She knew no English when she arrived and to the end of her days spoke it haltingly. But for some reason she suited George, now prepared to settle down and become a good family man.

Life at Charlotte's Court, even when she was not pregnant – she had fifteen children – sounds stultifyingly dull. One of the Queen's ladies-in-waiting chanced to be the extremely articulate Fanny Burney who gave a blow-by-blow account of the average day. It makes dull reading, but there is one point worth noting; while Queen Charlotte's hair was being dressed and powdered, made into one of those fantastic shapes which we simply accept as Georgian, the Queen *read the newspapers*. She was thus in touch with public opinion and at the end of a seemingly inactive day, could discuss things with George who was eager to reign properly, but seldom on good terms with his chief minister, and who was, in addition, beginning to suffer from a condition now known to be physical in origin but at the time thought to be mental derangement. When he had his first attack, his mother, still somebody to be reckoned with, tried to conceal the seriousness of his condition from his wife. But Charlotte *knew*. Not, of course, as we appear to know now; the disease called porphyria was only diagnosed and understood – partially – well into the middle of this century.

Both George and Charlotte had been reared to quiet living and preferred country to town life. There was Windsor Castle, but it had fallen into a sad state of disrepair; there was Hampton Court, but for George that was haunted by memories of the quarrels between his parents and his grand-parents. So, with a shy wife and the thought of raising a large family, the King bought, for the now laughable sum of £21,000, a pleasant suburban residence called Buckingham House which was renamed the 'Queen's House'. It is difficult now to think of it as semi-rural, but slow everything down to horse pace, think of Piccadilly as little more than a village and it is just possible to visualise the quiet, tree-surrounded retreat, not then as palatial as it is today. Here it was possible to indulge in something resembling family life such as George remembered at Kew.

The familiar Hanoverian pattern of dissention between father and son went on unbroken. How did George III, such a serious man, and one of such simple tastes that he rejoiced in the nickname of Farmer George, and his equally serious and very plain wife, come to produce such a Prince of Wales, so frivolous and so handsome? As with Henry VIII, George IV's youthful good looks have been lost in the image of a fat old man, but when he was young he was known as Prince Florizel.

Everything about him must have caused his parents the gravest concern. George III was a Tory – and an old-fashioned one at that – so his son must hob-nob with Whigs. He kept other company, too, raffish company, men who drank too much, gambled heavily and paid altogether too much attention to their clothes. It was in a way suitable that the arbiter of fashion in the Prince's circle should be the grandson of a valet – valets were supposed to know about the fitting of clothes, but although Beau Brummel had been schooled at Eton and been briefly at Oxford, he was not the man the royal parents would have chosen to be their son's closest companion. Brummel however could not be blamed for the Prince's worst misdemeanour, his secret – if secret it could be called – marriage to an actress, Mrs Fitzherbert. It had occurred before his time.

The very word actress still carried a faint hint of disrepute about it, but Mrs Fitzherbert, a widow of impeccable reputation, and a devout Roman Catholic, had refused absolutely to become the Prince's mistress; however she was fond of him, and when he threatened to commit suicide and did indeed make a token attempt at it, she wavered, went to his bedside and agreed to become his morganatic wife. A few words spoken, with due solemnity would satisfy her conscience and give him his heart's desire. She could never look forward with any certainty to the prospect of being Queen, since the Royal Marriage Act of 1772 made any marriage not given the consent of the ruling sovereign, invalid. But one day George, Prince of Wales would *be* ruling sovereign. . . . What then?

If the Prince of Wales really took that secret ceremony seriously he was prepared, in 1795, to commit bigamy. He had refurbished Carlton House – his residence since attaining his majority, and he had built – largely for Mrs Fitzherbert – a grand, half-oriental pavilion in the quiet little fishing village on the south coast, Brighthelmstone, now known as Brighton. The fashionable world flocked there – doctors had just become convinced that sea-bathing was a good thing.

Possibly George III, who had already had several warning signs that his health – or his sanity – was precarious, had chosen to forget his own infatuations; or chose only to look upon decent open marriage as a cure. And for anyone intent upon forcing the Prince of Wales into a decent open marriage there was a weapon to hand. His debts now amounted to £650,000. Parliament, less personally, but just as constitutionally concerned about the future of the dynasty – none of George's brothers had yet begotten a legitimate child – agreed to pay the Prince's debts, on condition that he married.

Another bride from one of those Protestant principalities which lay between Catholic France and Catholic Bavaria. This time Caroline of Brunswick.

The 'Queen's Palace' in 1803.

Caroline of Brunswick

Queen to George IV
born 1768, married 1795, died 1821

George, Prince of Wales was thirty-three years old in 1795, the year of his marriage, and from Mrs Fitzherbert onwards had shown a preference for elegant, sophisticated women, usually older than himself; the bride chosen for him was twenty-seven; just the wrong age, for the appeal which youth might have made to experience was lacking, so was the adaptability necessary to make a success of a marriage to which the bridegroom came most unwillingly.

Much has been made of Caroline's lack of physical attraction, but an impartial observer described her as not unpretty, with a fine high colour and a wealth of fair hair; she looked healthy enough, her movements were lively, if lacking in grace and it is reasonable to suppose that to her the marriage was welcome; twenty-seven was rather old by eighteenth-century standards and to be called from Brunswick to become Princess of Wales was an honour. Moreover she was not being married off to an entirely strange country. Her mother was George III's sister and therefore her husband-to-be was her cousin. One imagines that she came with goodwill.

It sounds extraordinary to us now, but it had taken Beau Brummel – the valet's grandson – to impose high standards of personal cleanliness upon the richest and the most fashionable. Brummel attained his ascendancy over the Prince of Wales at a time when it was still quite usual for a lady's hair to be dressed, smeared with pomade and powdered, fixed into a fantastic shape and then left alone for a week, ten days . . . Many most fashionable ladies were lousy. The heavy silks and velvets of their outer clothing could not be washed and body linen, being out of sight, could be in any state. There was a good deal of what is now called body odour, and that could be disguised by the lavish use of scent, the heavier and stronger the better.

Beau Brummel changed all that. He advocated frequent bathing of the whole body – the new Pavilion at Brighton included a bath as big as a swimming pool – and insisted that all linen, that next to the body as well as that visible, should be clean.

The cult of personal fastidiousness had not then reached Brunswick, and Lord Malmesbury, who had been sent to bring Caroline to England, said that she was 'smelly'; he persuaded one of her ladies so see that she had a good wash.

So it is unlikely that she was smelly when she confronted the Prince of Wales; he had sent his mistress-of-the-moment, Lady Jersey, to meet her at Greenwich, and there Lady Jersey had insisted that the bride-to-be should have a change of clothing – the new ones deliberately chosen to be as unbecoming as possible.

We read that at first sight of his bride the Prince staggered away, declaring that he was unwell and calling for brandy. And we have Caroline's own word for it that he spent the wedding night in the grate. He must have been very drunk, for he was a hedonist, and hedonists like comfort, but she said, 'Judge what it was to have a drunken husband on one's wedding day and one who passed the greatest part of his bridal night under the grate, where he fell and where I left him. If anybody say to me at dis moment – will you pass your life over again or be killed? I would choose death, for you know, a little sooner or later we must all die, but to live a life of wretchedness twice over – oh, mine God, no!'

There is something about that speech which indicates that she was not the insensitive hoyden that she is often made out to be. To a considerable extent what happened after was George's fault. He managed far less well than Henry VIII had done, faced with Anne of Cleves. Henry, so often called an ogre, suggested a brother-sister relationship and provided generously. George just managed to get Caroline pregnant, keep up some kind of facade until the child – a girl – was born, and then they parted.

It is a measure of the Prince's vast unpopularity that public sympathy was almost entirely with the Princess, despite the fact that she was a foreigner, not always resident in England, and that her behaviour was remarkably indiscreet. The English, with all their faults, show a tendency to side with anybody whom they consider to be ill-done-by.

The King and Queen must have suffered much mortification at the failure of the marriage which instead of settling and reforming George had simply led to more scandal. It had produced one *legitimate* grandchild, heir presumptive to the throne, and she bore the Queen's name, but the relationship between the Prince and his parents was not good enough for him to allow them any say in her upbringing. The Prince was not the man to make a good father, and the warm-hearted, lively little girl was brought up in seclusion, seeing her father at rare intervals, and her mother, when she was

A portrait of Caroline of Brunswick. Artist unknown.

in England, for about two hours a week.

There was another scandal within the family; Princess Sophia had a baby – unkind people said fathered by her brother, the Duke of Cumberland. Alternative sires were mentioned, but nobody was sure. George III, whose mind was already tottering, was kept in ignorance of it all; Princess Sophia's growing bulk and subsequent indisposition were explained to him as being the result of dropsy; and when she re-appeared she was said to have been cured by eating beef, which, as the King remarked, was an extraordinary thing.

His illness was becoming more serious. Sometimes he could not sleep; sometimes he slept and suffered nightmares; he had delusions, one being that he himself was dead; so he wore mourning for George III, that good man. There had been a time when he had described Queen Charlotte as his best doctor; now there were times when she dared not be left alone in a room with him.

In 1806, however, the King was sane enough to order an investigation into the behaviour of his daughter-in-law, the Princess of Wales. Much that was unsavoury was exposed; her behaviour had been indiscreet to the point of recklessness and her household now included two children, a boy and a girl, said to be adopted. But also in her household were two English ladies of unquestioned probity, who had been with her when she was abroad in Italy, and they testified that although she had been foolish she had never committed adultery.

Princess Charlotte was at an impressionable age when this inquiry took place – she was thirteen, old enough to have opinions of her own. She sided whole-heartedly with her mother. So did the English people who, when the acquittal was announced, put lights in every window – any window not lighted was liable to get a stone through it.

During the King's intermittent spells of so-called insanity, the Prince of Wales had acted as Regent and his immediate circle of friends had openly expressed their hope that George III would not recover. In 1810 their wish was granted. The King, then aged seventy-two, went into enforced retirement at Windsor, handed over to the care of doctors, some of whom believed that the insane should be treated kindly, some who held to more orthodox methods, whippings, starvation.

The Prince Regent – once his father was out of the way – became reconciled to his mother, and when she died in 1818, he was holding her hand.

With his wife no reconciliation was possible. Caroline had added to her faults by encouraging her daughter to rebel.

Charlotte – the victim of a broken marriage and always in need of the affection of which she had been deprived – enjoyed herself in her mother's household, ramshackle and un-royal as it was. She must have learned by that time that her mother was not to be relied upon to any great extent, and she believed that the two mysterious children, William Austin and Edwardina Kent were in fact Caroline's bastards; but at her mother's house she met exciting people and was allowed, without criticism, to exercise her taste for flirtation.

She was not a very stable character and would probably not have been a good Queen; she fell into love and out of it all too easily. She seemed to accept her father's proposal that she should marry Prince William of Orange, then changed her mind. She gave as her reason something calculated to touch every Englishman's heart – if she married William of Orange she would be obliged to leave England, her own country, her homeland which she loved.

It was all very dramatic, her flight in a hackney carriage to her mother's house; her father ordering her back, the promise of a suitor more to her taste, and one prepared to live in England, having no land of his own; Prince Leopold of Saxe-Coburg-Saalfeld. He was young and handsome and only too willing to accept Princess Charlotte, a guaranteed income of £50,000 a year and a beautiful residence at Claremont. (Later in his life he was elected King of the Belgians and was no mean power in European political life.)

The marriage, one is glad to read, was happy, but it ended in 1817, with Charlotte dead in childbirth, and her baby with her.

England would have no heir to the throne, unless one of the royal brothers could produce one. There was a slightly undignified rush to the altar.

*Caroline landing at Dover on her return to claim her rights
as Queen.*

In 1820 George III died and his son was King; fifty-eight years old, and
Caroline, still his legal wife, fifty-two, her child-bearing days done. What
of him? Admittedly he was not in very good physical shape, years of self-
indulgence had given him a stomach which had to be held into place by a
corset, but older and fatter men had been known to father children. We
cannot tell what was in George IV's mind when, immediately upon becoming King he ordered that Caroline's name should not be mentioned in the
liturgy; even in the humblest, most remote parish church she was not to
be prayed for; she must not be acknowledged as Queen. She was abroad at
the time, but she heard, recognised the insult, and came back to England,
ready to insist upon her rights. She had been even more indiscreet than ever;
once in Geneva she had gone to dance in a state now called topless, her
bosom, now of more than average size, exposed for all to see. Yet, when
George's advisers said that he now had ample grounds for divorce, the case
fell through. Every kind of criticism could be aimed at her behaviour; it
had been scandalous and disgraceful, but there was no more proof than on
a former occasion that she had committed adultery.

George could not divorce her; he could prevent her from being crowned.

Caroline did not think so; she had faith in the crowds who had greeted
her return to England with boisterous enthusiasm. She was misled. The mob
is notoriously fickle, and although during his attempt to divorce her George
had been so unpopular that his carriage was pelted with stones and filth,
suddenly public opinion swung in his favour. All the excitement and free

entertainment of the coronation was pending and something of the mystique of monarchy fell almost automatically upon the man about to be crowned. Also, although she had been acquitted of adultery, enough that was un-savoury had been revealed to make men ask themselves; Is this the kind of woman you would wish to have for a wife? The day came when, instead of being cheered in the streets she was jeered and hissed. People shouted 'Go back to Italy!' Italy had been the scene of her worst behaviour and an Italian had been named as her lover.

There was a streak of obstinacy in her; she made ready for the coronation and when the day came, regally robed and attended by faithful friends, she drove to Westminster Abbey only to find that door after door was closed against her. The King had given orders that she was not to be admitted. As she tried this entrance and then that, the crowd, so lately her friends, hooted and laughed. Utterly humiliated, she went home and within nineteen days was dead. Most accounts agree that the final rebuff broke her heart.

But why? Did the Crown of England mean so much to her?

There is another, just possible explanation. Her wedding night, by her own account, had been a disaster, but it had been followed by a brief honey-moon, during which her child had been conceived; and during the next nine months she had had time enough to fall under Prince Florizel's spell. He had a way with women; all his sisters adored him, so did some of his mistresses; Mrs Fitzherbert with whom he had broken temporarily before his marriage, asked and obtained Papal sanction to resume relationship with him afterwards.

If Caroline fell in love with him all her subsequent conduct is easily understandable; her behaviour, like that of a naughty child's, a bid for attention and all her indiscretions – stopping short of the ultimate act – were attempts to prove that she *was* attractive to men.

She died and her body was shipped back to Brunswick to lie with those of her family. George IV was free and he was King. He could, perhaps should, have acknowledged his marriage to Mrs Fitzherbert, so generally regarded as his wife that Caroline, defending herself against the charge of adultery, could say that the only adultery that she had ever committed was with the husband of Mrs Fitzherbert. Or, ignoring that secret marriage as he had ignored it when he married Caroline, he could have taken another bride. He did nothing. Perhaps he felt no need to for in a way the succession was assured. One of those hasty royal marriages – that of the Duke of Kent – had been productive and there was a little girl growing up in Kensington Palace. Her name was Victoria. And she remembered him, down the years; gross and gouty, the grease-paint on his face disgusting, but kindly and with wonderful dignity and charm of manner. And that rather supports the fancy that Caroline's heart was broken by a loss greater than that of the crowd's favour, or of the crown.

Adelaide
of Saxe-Meiningen

Queen to William IV
born 1792, married 1818, died 1849

Before Caroline of Brunswick's death, when the King appeared to be hope-
lessly entangled in a sterile marriage, people had begun to worry about the
succession. The King had several brothers, but none of them had yet produced a legitimate child. There was a spate of royal ducal marriages; among
them that of William, Duke of Clarence to Adelaide of Saxe-Meiningen.
He was fifty-three and not without sense; he wanted a bride young enough
to bear children, but not a silly young girl. Adelaide was twenty-six.

William had already proved that he could father children; his mistress –
an actress called Mrs Jordan had borne ten – he had been faithful to her. His
wife bore two, both girls and neither of them strong enough to survive the
dangers of infancy. So far as providing an heir went, William's marriage
had been an exercise in futility; but he had been fortunate in his choice; he
had a good wife.

People around the Court, long subject to the greed and insolence of
mistresses, thought it would be *nice* to have a Queen again, but at first sight
Adelaide, hitherto not much in the public eye, was a sad disappointment.
She was not merely plain but *frightful*, somebody wrote. Very ugly, with a
horrid complexion. As insignificant a little person as was ever seen. And so
ill-dressed! Her Leghorn straw hat was dyed, her muslin collar small and
shabby.

There was more in her than met the eye. She had great tolerance. Extremely moral herself, she accepted without quibble William's ten bastards, who
flocked into Windsor and every other royal residence, clamouring for
money, for titles. William was almost invariably indulgent. Once he *did*
refuse to pay a bill – £12,000 – owed by one of his sons, whereupon the
angry young man flounced off, taking with him twelve good horses, three
carriages and six servants – all belonging to his father.

*Francis Xavier Winterhalter has caught Adelaide's dowdiness
and respectability.*

It was not only William's sons who were demanding; he had sons-in-law
too; one of these, holding three important if somewhat obsolete-sounding
offices, refused to have his accounts inspected and, furious with his father,
turned upon Adelaide and abused her so violently that he made her cry.

William had spent most of his life in the Navy; he was popular, the bluff
Sailor King; but like many bluff men, he lacked tact. Surrounding himself

and his Queen with his bastards was tactless, and so was his recognition of Mrs Fitzherbert. Perhaps when they were all young together, George had confided in his brother; whether it was so or not, William invited her to Windsor, treated her as a most honoured guest, promised her an income of £6,000 a year and even gave her permission to deck out her servants in royal livery.

Adelaide went quietly on, actually laying the foundation of what was to be called the Victorian standard of morals and behaviour. She took great interest in the model cottages being built at Windsor and in the families – especially the children – who inhabited them. She was also kind to the little girl, growing up in Kensington Palace – Victoria – on the rare occasions when she was allowed to come to Court.

With the English people Queen Adelaide was never popular. She suffered, in a way, from William's popularity. The English wished to love their King; he was so different from his brother; the glamour of the Navy hung about him – Trafalgar was only twenty-five years distant – therefore when he took an unpopular attitude on any subject, people exonerated him and blamed his wife's influence. He opposed Parliamentary Reform and it was easy to think that their pleasant old Sailor King was not being stubbornly Tory, merely too much under his wife's thumb. In fact Adelaide took little interest in politics and when she and William spent a quiet evening together he gently dozed and she knitted. Sometimes, when he woke, in order to hide the fact that he had been asleep, he would say, 'Exactly so, Ma'am'. From such an innocent foible may have arisen the notion that he agreed with whatever she said.

Her choice of ladies-in-waiting added to the mistrust with which people regarded her; one was American, slightly related by marriage to the Bonaparte family; another was a devout Catholic. England had been at war with America in 1812, and at war with the head of the Bonaparte clan until 1815, so that lady-in-waiting was disliked on two counts. As for the Catholic! Just at a time when Catholic Emancipation was a red-hot issue, with red-hot tempers on both sides. But both these gossipped-about ladies were of the utmost respectability, part of a very respectable and rather dull Court and Victoria's mother – the Duchess of Kent – had little reason for her pretence that it was not a fit place for her daughter to frequent.

Over the Reform Bill William quarrelled violently with his ministers, and though compelled to deal with them where government was concerned, refused absolutely to entertain them as guests. Private family parties were a different matter and on 13 August 1836 Queen Adelaide's birthday was to be celebrated. The French chefs who had ruled the royal kitchens during George IV's reign had all been dismissed and drunkenness was no longer the fashion, though William disliked anybody who did not drink wine. Everything was set up for the proper celebration of the Queen's birthday and naturally the Duchess of Kent and her daughter, heir apparent, were invited. They were asked to come to Windsor for the Queen's birthday and stay on to celebrate the King's which fell eight days later.

The Duchess of Kent ignored the invitation to Adelaide's birthday party, but indicated that she and Victoria would be at Windsor for the King's birthday.

Whether their absence from the birthday party of a woman who was capable of taking her knitting to Ascot and remarking that some horses were sure to win, was serious is questionable; their presence, eight days later, provoked King William into making a most extraordinary speech. He stood up – the Duchess of Kent sitting at his right hand, and Victoria directly opposite – and said, 'I trust in God that my life may be spared for nine months longer, after which period, in the event of my death, no regency would take place'. He spoke of his desire to leave authority 'to that young lady', and pointed to his niece. He rambled on about having been grossly and repeatedly insulted by 'a person now near me'. The young lady, he complained, had always been kept away from his Court, but in future things would be different. 'I shall insist and command that the Princess do upon all occasions appear at my Court, as it is her duty to do'.

By the end of it Victoria was crying and Queen Adelaide so deeply distressed as to seem upon the point of collapse. The Duchess of Kent was unmoved and immediately after the dinner announced her departure.

Some people thought that this speech, whatever the provocation had been, and William's increasing hostility to officials – 'You had better go home and learn to read!' – heralded an onset of his father's madness; but he stayed of sound mind, though of failing health, for the period he had asked of God. In May 1837 Victoria reached the age of eighteen – for royal personages full age – and less than four weeks later William, as though no more was required of him, quietly died. Even some of his death-bed talk concerned the niece who was to succeed him, and showed an extraordinary percipience, in an unpercipient man. 'It will touch every sailor's heart to have a girl Queen to fight for. They'll be tattooing her face on their arms and I'll be bound they'll all think she was christened for Nelson's ship'.

Adelaide outlived her husband by twelve years. She could no longer be blamed for unpopular political decisions, and if she had ever feared – as it would have been natural to do – any further humiliating snubs from the rude Duchess of Kent, she lived to see that they were unfounded. Victoria's mother was to suffer almost total eclipse; and when the young Queen married she chose a man of family and background practically identical with Adelaide's own.

She was buried at Windsor, but her real memorial is elsewhere. The capital of South Australia, and by far the biggest, most flourishing port in the whole Continent, bears the name of this modest and self-effacing woman.

$\mathcal{V}ictoria$

Queen in her own right
born 1819, married 1840, died 1901

Is there, indeed, anything left to be said about her?

Countless people have written about her; she wrote about herself – she was one of the most prolific letter-writers in an age when everybody wrote letters; she kept a diary and published extracts from it. Can the most determined mangle squeeze out a single drop of juice?

One can say that she was one of the least understood women in history and that much of the misunderstanding was created by those who admired her most; so busy representing her as a model of all the virtues that they lost sight of the real woman. For Victoria to have become as she is all too often made to seem would have required a very massive operation – every drop of Hanoverian blood would have had to be drained from her veins and milk-and-water substituted. The real woman had a sense of humour, and if she ever made that famous remark, 'We are not amused', it was because there was nothing at which to be amused. She was once obliged to ask Mr Gladstone not to address her as though she were a public meeting, and he cannot have been the only bore she encountered. The real woman, the one behind the matriarch, loathed being pregnant, and made no secret of the fact; she did not even like to hear that anyone she cared for was in that state. Many women of her own child-bearing generation had cause to thank her for as soon as chloroform was available she insisted upon having it to ease the pangs of childbirth – and that was at a time when many clerics and other men regarded such pains as the fulfilment of God's threat to Eve. The real woman was fond of men; she liked them; there is an undercurrent of sexual attraction, blameless and never acknowledged, in her relationship with two of her Prime Ministers, Lord Melbourne and Mr Disraeli, and with Napoleon III. It was singularly fortunate that she found, so early in life, a man she could love, a man capable of dominating her. And when he was dead and the Queen had gone into everlasting mourning, there was John Brown, masculine, earthy, sometimes rude, but somebody unlikely to drop dead of shock at the discovery that she liked whisky and was not above enjoying the occasional, surreptitious cigarette.

The real woman is so much more engaging than the image. In some ways she was well ahead of her time. She had at least an instinct for genetics and though fair herself, would have preferred her son to marry a dark-haired princess who would bring a strain of new blood into the family. Few of her contemporaries would have put it so bluntly. It is a pity that her name should become so synonymous with stuffiness, piety carried to the edge of hypocrisy, exaggerated grief and all the rest of it. I do not think that the real Victoria would turn in her grave were it said that the Victorian age shaped her, rather than she it.

She was born as a result of the scramble by the brothers of George IV to produce an heir. Only her father, the Duke of Kent – married to another German Princess, Victoria Maria Louisa of Saxe-Coburg – succeeded. He died when his child was young and Victoria was brought up by her mother, a cantankerous character. But Victoria had a reasonably happy childhood, though isolated. Queen Adelaide's reputation was flawless, and under her influence – and that of increasing age – William IV had completely reformed, but the Duchess of Kent insisted upon regarding the Court as a corrupt and immoral place. When it became obvious that Victoria would succeed him, William IV offered to adopt her; an offer scornfully rejected.

It is certain that the Duchess of Kent, and her friend and adviser, Sir John Conroy, had another motive in keeping Victoria far away from any in-fluence but their own: if they could keep her young for her age, unsophisti-cated, reliant upon them they would have great power when she ascended the throne.

They misread her entirely. Early in the morning of 20 June 1837 – a month all but four days after her eighteenth birthday, she was informed that her uncle was dead. And somewhere in that crowded day she made a very revealing arrangement; hitherto she had always slept in her mother's room. That night she slept in one of her own.

She had always hated Sir John Conroy; and although the fashion of the day had demanded at least a pretence at filial affection in a well-behaved girl, her behaviour during the next three years indicated that she was not truly fond of her mother. The Duchess of Kent could take her place at her daughter's table, and in her daughter's drawing-room, but she was never treated as a confidante or given any proof of affection.

Queen Anne with the poor little Prince William, Duke of Gloucester, painted by Godfrey Kneller.

The young Queen, small and slight, very fair, appealed to the English people and her coronation was splendid. Less than two years after it Victoria learned how fickle the mob could be; those who had flung flowers as she went to be crowned, were flinging stones at her carriage when she took an outing. And all on account of Lady Flora Hastings, a lady-in-waiting.

On the surface a simple, tragic story – too often retold; but its roots lay deeper. Lady Flora, eminently respectable and more than ordinarily intelligent and cultivated, had been introduced into Kensington Palace, as lady-in-waiting to the Duchess of Kent, in the hope that she would prove to be an agreeable companion to the young Princess, whose affection seemed to centre too much upon her former governess, Baroness Lehzen. Lady Flora made the incredible mistake of siding with Sir John Conroy against Baroness Lehzen who was one of the people whom Victoria truly loved. So, when the two households were more or less combined and Lady Flora *looked* pregnant, and had committed another error, having once travelled in a coach alone with Conroy, she found no friend in the Queen; nor in the Queen's official physician, Sir James Clark who, after a pretty cursory examination, suggested hopefully that she might be secretly married.

Taking what was, after all, no more than the ordinary attitude towards such scandals, and in addition bearing a very old grudge against Sir John Conroy, and one of less age but lively enough against Lady Flora, Victoria took Lady Flora's guilt for granted; but when a closer examination showed that a tumour on the liver was responsible for the pregnant appearance, the Queen hastened to make amends and made a visit to the sick-bed which proved to be a death-bed. Scandal however has faster feet than truth and Victoria was unpopular for a time.

Victoria had an uncle on her mother's side. He was the busiest busy-body in Europe. He had married Charlotte, George IV's daughter, who died bearing his dead child; he still drew the income settled upon him at the time of his marriage; and he had been elected to be King of the Belgians. He still liked to have a finger in every pie, and saw, in a marriage to the Queen of England, a great chance for his nephew, Albert, Victoria's cousin, came to England on a visit, took the Queen's eye and then, on a later visit, her heart, and within a few months was married to her and launched on a career so frustrating that he died, a weary, disillusioned man, at the age of forty-two.

Albert the Good.

Good he certainly was; and certainly Victoria loved him; but few of her subjects did. They considered him – with his music and his learning – a high-brow, never a popular thing to be. And they considered him mean. He had an orderly mind, he came from a relatively poor Court and he tried to

Queen Charlotte in 1780 by Benjamin West. Thirteen of her fifteen children can be seen in front of Windsor Castle.

reduce Victoria's household expenses while speeding up the process by which a broken window could be mended. And who had a more spiteful tongue than a sacked housemaid, or a man who had lost a sinecure? One must suspect that some of the over-used stories about the private life of Victoria and Albert, the quarrels and arguments, came from prejudiced sources.

Once he did a mean thing in public. In his well-intentioned way he took an interest in agriculture and entered some beast he had bred in a show; it won a prize, some trivial sum, and Albert put it into his own pocket, not into that of the stockman who held the halter. Could anything be more despicable?

Who remembers him for his work on the re-housing of the poor? Or for the part he played in organising the famous Great Exhibition of 1851 to which the whole world flocked in the wonderful Crystal Palace? Who, entering the Albert Hall for this reason or that, thinks of it as his memorial?

Despite the Queen's dislike of being pregnant and her perfectly rational fear of childbirth she endured the process nine times and produced four sons and five daughters. The typical Victorian family, but like all such, one with some rifts. Victoria's first child was a daughter, named after her, but called Vicky, a very intelligent, even precocious little girl in whose education the Prince Consort took great interest and sometimes a hand.

It is an acknowledged fact that fathers tend to favour their daughters, mothers, their sons, and it is likely that had Victoria's second child, Edward, been anything like a match for his sister in his ability to learn from books, his mother would have favoured him more, holding better cards in the age-old game of Your Daughter, My Son. As it was, Edward and his mother were at a disadvantage. Edward tried hard but lessons bored him; he was interested, not in books, but in people and things; he was quite as clever as his sister, but in a different way, so his parents chose to call him stupid.

In many ways Victoria was a good mother; with Edward she failed as two rather sorry little stories prove. Once this keenly observant little boy asked whether a pink was the female of a carnation. Anybody who had seen the two flowers, so similar, but the pink so small, the carnation so large, would have considered this a rational, even praiseworthy question; but with Edward, no, a silly question, proof of stupidity and perhaps – perhaps a deplorable, precocious interest in sex.

And when Edward was fourteen he went with his parents to visit France where Napoleon III and his Empress kept a very gay Court. The Emperor

Victoria, aged fifteen, with her mother, the Duchess of Kent.
Engraving by Beechy.

was no match for Albert in looks, or in worthiness, but when the time came to leave Edward said, with feeling, 'I wish I were *your* son'. Not the remark of a happy boy.

Over the marriages of her children Victoria showed a most un-Victorian and un-royal leniency; allowing them a most unusual amount of choice. And she disapproved of princesses marrying too young. The Crown Prince of Prussia came on a visit and was greatly attracted by Vicky who reciprocated his feeling. It was, on the face of it, a good match and Vicky was mature for her age; most mothers would have snatched at it but Victoria refused to permit the marriage until her daughter was eighteen. It was as well that she did; the poor girl had a few more happy years before going to Prussia where, except for her husband's love, everything combined to make her wretched.

Victoria's mother died in 1861 and Victoria mourned her with vigour; Albert had long ago brought about a reconciliation between mother and daughter, but there may have been enough remorse to spur the grief.

In that same year Edward, Prince of Wales, reached the age of twenty; and his behaviour was causing concern. He went for a short time to Ireland to join a regiment in which he held an honorary commission, and like most young officers, he had a very fleeting affair with a young woman.

Victoria and Albert had always been haunted by the fear that their son, very handsome, uncommonly charming, might revert to the terrible pattern of his Hanoverian great-uncles; now it seemed that their fear was well-founded.

By the time that the gossip reached his parents Edward was installed at Cambridge, not as an ordinary undergraduate but in a great house nearby. Thither, on a cold winter's day, Albert must go to administer a lecture. The Prince Consort was already suffering from a heavy cold, which the train journey and the emotional upset did nothing to improve; he came home, took to his bed and died on 14 December 1861. What ailed him was never completely certain; probably typhoid fever, said the people who thought the sanitation even of palaces far from satisfactory; the complications following a heavy cold in a man never robust and suffering from depression; a lack of will to live.

By her subsequent behaviour towards her son and heir, Victoria seemed to show that to an extent she held him to blame. He was twenty; two years older than she had been when she was crowned, but although from Albert's death to her own she complained, often querulously, about the burden which affairs of state imposed upon her, she made no attempt to share the load with Edward. He was allowed to take on his father's work for good causes and to delegate for his mother in the social life which no woman in mourning could possibly be expected to endure, but of the day-to-day routine of government in the country over which he was one day to reign,

*Queen Victoria with the Prince Consort and five of her children
in 1846, by Winterhalter.*

he knew no more than any man in the street. Even when, towards the end,
the Queen grew purblind, she still held the reins; aided by Princess Beatrice
who read to her, and by her own phenomenal memory.

Her seclusion made life difficult for her ministers; in the forty years after
Albert's death she visited London only seven times – so those who wished
to advise or consult her had a great deal of travelling to do. Her favourite
residences were Balmoral and Osborne, both planned by Albert.

After a time the ordinary people began to think that this mourning
period was being unduly prolonged. Even nowadays, with so many other
competing entertainments, any kind of royal procession can draw a crowd;
a hundred years ago the Queen's absence from her capital was more keenly
felt. The Prince of Wales had married Alexandra with whom everybody
fell in love at first sight; why did not the Queen abdicate; hand over to the
young?

Those who considered it even as a mere possibility, underestimated
Victoria; just as the elegant French had underestimated her on her first visit
to Paris, thinking her clothes dowdy and her over-sized reticule, embroidered

Queen Victoria in old age with one of her dogs. A woodcut by
William Nicholson.

with a poodle, ridiculous; within a few hours they had learned what being
royal meant; she might wear frumpish clothes, and far too many jewels to
be elegant, but she was royal; a woman born to be Queen.

Queen; then Empress of India, she ruled, by strictly constitutional
methods, the greatest area of the world's surface ever to be welded into one
unit. She lived to enjoy that reverence so often accorded to the old. A
Golden Jubilee; a Diamond Jubilee, both celebrations to put any former
ones into the shade.

She died, as many old people do, painlessly and peacefully; having
reigned for four years longer than any other British monarch. And she
went to her grave followed by a larger concourse of royal personages than
had ever been seen before, or would be seen again. An epoch had ended.

Alexandra
of Denmark
Queen to Edward VII
born 1844, married 1863, died 1925

Great care had to be exercised over the choice of a wife for Edward. It was no longer necessary to find a princess with a large dowry, or to make a match for political reasons, but it was essential that whoever was chosen should be beautiful, indeed very beautiful in order to win and, if possible, retain, the Prince's affection; she must be good-natured, resolutely cheerful, gay without being flighty, dignified even in trying circumstances. Where was such a paragon to be found? And when found, how could it be manoeuvred so that it seemed as though the Prince had chosen her himself? Both Albert and Victoria knew their son well enough to understand that he was inclined to be contrary and resentful of coercion.

The Crown Princess of Prussia was asked to help in this search – and to find if possible, a dark-haired beauty. In that she failed, but she sent her parents photographs of Alexandra and although Victoria was not enthusiastic about the Princess's family – she thought them flighty – the photographs were impressive.

Albert lived just long enough to know that his clever eldest daughter had arranged for her brother and Alexandra to be introduced as though by accident, but he died before Edward had reached a final decision.

In the next year, 1862, Victoria put grief aside for long enough to go to Laeken in Belgium and see Alexandra for herself. She still did not like the parents much but she was impressed both by Alexandra's looks and by her general demeanour.

Not since Katharine of Aragon had the English people fallen so thoroughly and lastingly in love with a foreign princess as they did with Alexandra. (The late Princess Marina of Kent, related to her by blood, was very like her, so we do not have to rely upon static photographs or upon descriptions.) The public would have liked a great wedding in London, but Victoria was still in mourning and it was a quiet wedding at Windsor.

After the wedding, which took place in March 1863, Queen Victoria was not missed socially; there was the Prince of Wales, with looks of his own, and charm of his own, and there was the lovely Princess, so enchanting that many men, including her brother-in-law, fell in love with her. She was physically equipped for a tiring role; she had had an unusual upbringing; her father believed that girls as well as boys should practise gymnastics. On one occasion she stood, with only a short break, through 3,000 presentations. Even pregnancy did not put an end to her social activities. She was even able to ignore the first twinges of labour pains; the baby was not due for another two months; so she made nothing of it, and it took Lady Macclesfield – mother of thirteen children – to realise what was happening. She took charge, called the nearest doctor and wrapped the baby – England's heir – weighing only $3\frac{1}{2}$ lbs in her own flannel petticoat, nothing else being ready. Queen Victoria chose this little boy's name, Albert Victor Christian Edward, a sequence which is said to have annoyed his father.

Alexandra began to go deaf quite early in life; the condition may have been hereditary; her mother was deaf, but in her later years. One is inclined to wonder, now that a little more is known about the mind's control of the body. One asks why nothing positive was done about this deafness; no ear-trumpet – an old device; no tube of cardboard – effective in many cases; with another woman similarly afflicted, Alexandra tried to learn to lip-read – and made no progress.

Is it possible that she did not *want* to hear? Did she begin to turn a deaf ear during the dispute between Denmark and Prussia over the Duchies of Schleswig-Holstein? Her one known comment at the time was, 'the Duchies belong to Papa'. Whatever arguments followed, all in favour of Prussia, she did not wish to hear. Nor did she wish, later on, to hear the rumours of Edward's infidelities. It would be idle now to pretend that he was a faithful husband.

Experienced men warn younger men against marrying a woman for her looks; one becomes indifferent to them as one becomes indifferent to the most beautiful picture on one's own wall. And some men simply are not monogamous animals. Edward was one of the non-monogamous kind. The marriage stayed firm; another son, George – later to be George V of England – was born in 1865, and two years later, Princess Louise. That birth coincided with an attack of rheumatic fever which left Alexandra with a permanently stiff knee, something else to be ignored as far as such a handicap could be, though it put an end to the frolicsome, rather childish romps which she had so much enjoyed – probably as an antidote to the dignity so often demanded of her in public life. Not that she was, even at her most dignified, cold and unresponsive; she had a ready smile, a willingly waving hand.

Parliament had granted the young couple an income of £40,000 a year, in addition to what the Duchy of Cornwall yielded, but they always over-

*A formal painting of Queen Alexandra which nevertheless
portrays her enchantment, by Luke Fildes.*

spent their income. Many of Edward's chosen friends were newly rich men
with much larger incomes, and Alexandra had no money sense at all and
was in addition wildly generous. Told that a gift she proposed to give was
too large, she would receive the rebuke with a smile, and then double the
gift. She loved jewels and Edward gave her so many that Queen Victoria
was forced to protest; Alexandra had enough jewels, already. (Amongst
her jewels was a necklace of opals and diamonds with a slightly macabre
touch about it – it had been a wedding gift from the Prince Consort who
was dead, but not, Victoria insisted, ever to be forgotten.)

*A photograph of Alexandra playing cards with her parents,
the King and Queen of Denmark, and the Duchess of
Cumberland.*

Alexandra had always taken religion seriously and this tendency increased
as she grew older and she needed comfort where it could be found. She
might turn a deaf ear to rumour, and she did not care for reading books,
but she could hardly escape the newspapers and know that Edward had
been involved – though not as co-respondent – in a divorce case, and in a
card-sharping scandal, though there again he was not the guilty one. He was
rapidly losing popularity when a near-fatal attack of typhoid fever swung
public sentiment towards him again. When he recovered Thanksgiving
Services were held everywhere, except in some intensely non-conformist
communities – the spiritual offspring of the Puritans.

Meanwhile children were growing up and a bride must be found for the
heir, Prince Albert Victor, Duke of Clarence, that tiny baby so prematurely
born. Physically he had caught up; he had great charm, but he lacked the
ability to concentrate, and when, with his younger brother George, he had
been sent to undergo some naval training, opinions of him were as bad as
those of his brother were good. Eddie, as they called him had already shown
an interest in women, and some fickleness; so the best thing to do was to

marry him quickly. The Queen, growing old, the Prince and Princess of Wales, nudging middle-age, were agreed that the proper wife for Eddie was Princess Mary of Teck, who, despite her German-sounding name, was an Englishwoman by upbringing.

The young couple became engaged in December 1891, and early in the New Year there was to be a grand family party at Sandringham – that ugly new house in Norfolk which Edward had acquired as a private dwelling, much as his mother had taken to Balmoral and Osborne. The Teck family arrived not in the best of health; a cold? Think nothing of it! Influenza? A nuisance, but not deadly. However it killed the heir to the throne. It may be that his bad physical start in life had left a weakness and that his poor record in the Navy, his disinclination to concentrate, even his fickleness towards women were symptomatic. Nature is even now an underestimated force; there may have been, inside this unfortunate young man, an instinctive knowledge that he had no time to waste.

Alexandra held his hand as he died; and who knows? That sad experience may have inspired her determination to see that other women's sons should be cared for as far as possible. Almost as soon as she was Queen she established a special branch of a military nursing service, women who held rank and exercised a good deal of authority. She also supported ordinary hospitals and the International Red Cross, and she did not shrink from visiting patients, however distressing their appearance might be. On one occasion she looked at and talked to a man suffering from the most disfiguring disease – elephantiasis – a stricken man from whom most people preferred to avert their gaze.

Princess Mary of Teck had seemed to be the ideal wife for the Prince who had died; it seemed to everybody that she would be equally suitable for his brother George. She became engaged to him later that year. This was not quite the I-will-be-Queen-of-England-at-all-costs decision which it may appear to be to the superficial eye. We cannot know how much persuasion went on privately; we cannot assess Mary's own feelings. It is plain that she and Eddie had had little time to become fond of one another in the way that comes from very close acquaintance. It is equally clear, from the success of the marriage between Mary and George, that they were well suited. Mary was probably happier with George, a man of solid worth, than she would have been with Eddie, despite his charm.

After the marriage of George and Mary – it took place in 1893 – Alexandra's position was a frustrating one; she was still beautiful, and indeed remained so into extreme old age, but she was no longer young; she was deaf and slightly lame; she was caught as it were between the old Queen and the young Duchess of York. This may account for a certain arbitrariness which crept into her behaviour; if opposed in any way she would say, 'It is my wish. That is sufficient'. She was reluctant to give way to Mary or to

Alexandra taking a rose named after her from a child in 1912.
These roses are still sold in aid of hospitals and nurses.

delegate any little office or duty to her. This has sometimes been construed as jealousy; it could have been mere self-defence.

Edward's situation was even worse as the century aged. He had performed punctiliously every trivial duty entrusted to him but he was absolutely excluded from anything of a political nature; never consulted about any major matter concerning the country over which he would one day reign. He had his consolations, his mistresses, his friends, his trips abroad, his race-horses – he owned three Derby winners – and his yacht.

Alexandra spent more and more time at Sandringham, her favourite home, surrounded by her pet animals. But she was not a recluse. When the well-known Alexandra roses were first sold in the streets in aid of hospitals and nurses – then not state-supported – she made a point of speaking personally to as many sellers as was possible.

Victoria died, full of years and honours, in January 1901.

Victoria and Alexandra had been friendly, with reservations on both sides; Victoria thought Alexandra allowed her children too much freedom and Alexandra strongly disapproved of John Brown, to give only two instances, but Alexandra had always shown herself very sympathetic to anyone in any kind of sorrow and no doubt she shared England's feeling of loss at the death of the old Queen who had become a legend in her life-time.

Still there was the coronation to come.

That was the coronation which almost did not happen.

Edward had felt unwell, had suffered some warning pains but struggled on manfully until two days before the long-awaited day. Then he succumbed to a condition which throughout the ages had killed a lot of people; known as inflammation of the bowel. Now they knew better and there was a surgeon ready to remove Edward's appendix. He was a bold man, Sir Frederick Treves, for this particular operation was new, and if it went wrong . . .

However it went right and within a fortnight Edward was convalescent and in August 1903, he and Alexandra went to their coronation in Westminster Abbey.

Alexandra was fifty-six, Edward three years older. She had kept her figure and her looks, and dressed in a frock of Indian golden gauze and with a crown of diamonds on her head she was still sufficiently beautiful to make a quite disinterested bystander say that she was the loveliest woman he had ever seen.

Alexandra was Queen for so short a time – only nine years, during which she continued all her charitable works and also, probably without direct intention, showing that a court in order to be virtuous need not be deadly dull. She could spend the day organising relief for the unemployed – there were some even then – and in the evening preside at a reception very different from the dreary 'drawing-rooms' of the past. And when Edward lay dying, somewhat unexpectedly of what had seemed to be a mere chill, Alexandra made a gesture of exceptional magnanimity. He had had a number of mistresses, the actress Lillie Langtry among them, but his current love was a Mrs Keppel. Alexandra sent for her to be at his death-bed. What further proof of love could a woman give?

She lived on, through troubled times; the first Great War during which the nursing services inaugurated by her and then copied proved their worth. She read, if she did not hear, about the revolution in Russia and the slaughter of her relatives in a cellar at Ekaterinberg. She was not in London on the night of wild celebration on Armistice night 1918, but she was there when Haig made his triumphal entry, and she gave him a flower.

Of her grandchildren she particularly favoured George's eldest son, called in the family David, who had inherited much of her beauty and all of her charm. Whether she would have approved of his love affair with Mrs Simpson is debatable. She might have done, for she was, beyond any other quality, tolerant.

She died in 1925, suddenly and easily of a heart attack and was buried beside Edward, at Windsor, a place which had never appealed to her much.

Mary of Teck

Queen to George V
born 1867, married 1893, died 1955

To a degree this little girl, born in the same bedroom as Queen Victoria had been, and almost on the old Queen's birthday, was capable of introducing the desired strain of new blood. Her grandfather, Duke of Württemberg had married for love, a beautiful, but un-royal Hungarian Countess. This unorthodox act which was to be curiously echoed three generations later – disqualified his children from succeeding. Princess Mary's father made his home in England, married a cousin of Queen Victoria's, and the Queen was godmother to the child who was christened Victoria Mary.

Despite this relationship, there was something of a Cinderella about Mary in her early days. Her family knew periods of comparative poverty, largely due to the mismanagement of what money was available; and almost everyone with whom Mary came in contact had grander titles. As a result she became extremely shy, a condition not alleviated by her mother's continual harping on it. However, when the time came to look about for a bride for Eddie, the elder son of the Prince of Wales, Mary had, in Victoria's eyes, one advantage quite apart from her own gifts and looks. Three strong, healthy brothers. Plainly she came from good breeding stock. Mary was briefly engaged to Eddie, and when he died, soon engaged, and then married, to his brother George.

As Alexandra may have felt herself caught in a frustrating situation between the ageing Queen and the young Duchess of York, so the Duchess of York may have felt herself caught between Victoria, rapidly becoming a legend in her life-time, and Alexandra, still so beautiful. Of her own looks she had a small opinion; her hair was fair, her eyes very blue, but she thought that she too much resembled George III's Charlotte to be pretty; though she was proud of her descent on one side from the English royal family.

*The young Princess Mary of Teck who was affianced to two
heirs to the throne.*

She had enjoyed a better-than-average education and the gay frivolous
circle of the Prince and Princess of Wales thought her dull because she was
intellectually inclined. What nobody could ever quibble about was her
dignity; and in a curious way her husband, with his hatred of change, contributed towards the making of that very dignified, slightly awesome front
which she presented to the world. He was one of the generation to whom a
shortening of skirts, or of hair, spelt decadence.

Within a year of their marriage Mary bore what everybody had hoped
for – 'a very strong boy, a pretty child', as Victoria described him. Edward
Albert Christian George Andrew Patrick David – the one who later was to
cause his mother so much grief; and seventeen months later Mary had a
second son, Albert Frederick Arthur George. Her third child was Mary, the
Princess Royal; two other sons followed.

Mary had hated pregnancy and all to do with it as heartily as Victoria had
done and if her behaviour can be faulted – whose cannot? – it is in the
inefficient supervision which she exercised over her children's early years.
Admittedly she was a busy woman, but she did not give her nursery the
intimate attention which was badly needed. When the cheerful little boy
called David was brought down to meet his parents, the nurse gave him a
sharp pinch, so that he cried and both his mother and father regarded him
as a whining, lachrymose child and said, 'Take him away', which was just

what the nurse wanted. His brother suffered more; his legs were not straight enough and he had to wear braces on them, by day and by night though he begged to be released at night. And he was born left-handed; made to use his right hand, he developed a stammer. Both boys were given those fierce purgative doses which can ruin all but the strongest constitution. David went, apparently, unscathed, but Bertie suffered a weak digestion and stomach-pains to the end of his life. Finally the woman who had had charge of them had a breakdown which revealed that she had been a bit mad for quite a long time.

Of the dead let nothing but good be spoken; but surely somebody – and who if not the mother? – should have taken a little more interest. Yet her innate kindness and will-to-good were never in question and both were displayed to the utmost during the First World War, when, with or without her husband, she visited hospitals, convalescent homes, munition factories.

Not since George II had fought at the Battle of Dettingen had a King of England stood on a battlefield and from the horrible sight of freshly wounded men Queens had been spared even longer; now, with the war only just across the Channel, and all communications speeded up, the results of war were all too visible. Hospitals must be visited, unflinchingly, and with a smile. It is not surprising that Queen Mary took a very active interest in the improvement of artificial limbs, or that King George should write to her – 'If it wasn't for you I should break down'. In many ways he appeared to dominate her, but he depended upon her, too.

Both King George and Queen Mary took the war very seriously; when food was rationed, they rationed themselves; they ate potatoes which had grown in what had been their flower-beds; they banished alcohol completely. Given their own way, they would have turned Buckingham Palace into a hospital – but the authorities rejected that idea.

In what little time she had to spare Queen Mary headed salvage drives; horse chestnuts – good for some chemical process now that glycerine was scarce; empty jam-jars, scrap iron. Occasionally she would rescue from a field what looked like a bit of discarded iron, but was in fact a vital piece of some farmer's machinery. In such a case one of her retinue would smuggle it back.

So far as she could she kept peace within the family – a Herculean task. The word *gay* has now been debased, but Mary's first-born was gay in the old sense of the word, and gaiety was one thing his father conspicuously lacked. There is a touching little story of the King coming across David trying to teach his mother a new dance step and expressing his disapproval so violently that she never tried again. To somebody in his private life so

Queen Elizabeth the Queen Mother on her seventy-fifth birthday,
photographed by Norman Parkinson.

strongly conservative as George V, even in the matter of clothes, his elder son must have been a problem and a puzzle. He was so like what George IV had been in his youth – Prince Florizel; unbelievably good-looking, completely charming – his tours of the Empire had been overwhelming successes; but, like his grandfather, Edward VII, he liked bright lights, witty company – irrespective of origin; and inside him, not immediately evident, was the stubborn, Hanoverian streak, combined with an unconventionality which seemed to be dangerous to those in power and eventually spelt out his doom.

Those old enough to remember the gossip may recall how it was said that David, Prince of Wales was violently opposed to his sister's marriage to an English nobleman of undisputed worth, very rich, but her senior by some years and not very attractive physically. If indeed he did protest, as at the time he was said to do, his protests were over-ridden.

Time went on. Queen Mary – possibly because she had known what it meant to be poor when she was young – got on exceptionally well with the leaders of the growingly powerful Trade Unions, and with the first Labour Prime Minister, Ramsay MacDonald. The King accepted him too, saying that fourteen years in the Navy had given him some experience of people; but Mary's approach was more personal; she had been supporting any cause in favour of working women – even to homes where they could go and convalesce after an illness – since long before the war. Gandhi, in loincloth and slippers, she accepted.

Years and years of acceptance and in the end something absolutely unacceptable.

It is difficult now, forty tumultuous years later, to understand the horror which attached itself to the word divorce in the thirties. Even the so-called innocent party was smeared by association, and here was the heir to the throne paying serious attentions to a woman who had been through the divorce court once, and must go again if he really intended to marry her, for her second husband was still alive. How soon and how much did his parents know when in the summer of 1935 they celebrated the Silver Jubilee of their reign, an event enthusiastically shared even by people in the depressed areas? The King and Queen were so personally popular that the government of the day had once asked them to make a tour of likely trouble spots – it had been effective, for a time; and the Silver Jubilee brought a touch of colour and gaiety to even the drabbest of streets, with little flags and strings of bunting hanging where ordinarily the washing flapped, and below the decorations, children making merry over sandwiches and buns – sometimes provided by benevolent town councils, sometimes by private benefactors and sometimes by the street-dwellers themselves.

A happy picture of the Queen in 1975.

Even the grounds at Windsor were turned over to produce food;
Queen Mary watches her husband digging in 1917.

In some of the photographs taken in that day, George V looks old and unwell; he was seventy, had had several illnesses – once it had been rumoured that he was dead and crowds had thronged outside the gates of Buckingham Palace. Mary was only two years younger, but upright as ever, armoured in dignity, in graciousness, in self-control and the kind of clothing which had ceased to be merely old-fashioned, and become something singularly individual.

The King died in January 1936, at Sandringham, the place he loved best. Mary had summoned the family, but in carefully worded messages, so that George should not suspect that they had been called to his death-bed. And when the King died, she was the first to kiss the hand of her eldest son; he was King and she was his subject. Not David I of England, but Edward VIII.

On a murky winter day, George V's coffin went from Sandringham to Wolferton station; followed on that bit of the journey by his favourite pony, Jock, on whom he had taken a doddering little ride, supported by Mary, only three days before he died. And in Westminster Hall, where he lay in state, his four sons took a spell of sentinel duty; the King, the Duke of York, the Duke of Gloucester and the Duke of Kent.

About Edward and Mrs Simpson the English press had been honourably silent, and papers coming in from America had been censored, pages cut out, or blacked out. But people travelled between England and America, between England and the Continent, and they talked. Everybody knew, in a vague way. And soon the truth was out – or as much of it as was thought acceptable. Was his real exit line, 'I am going to marry Mrs Simpson and I am prepared to go', or had he dismissed himself earlier, under a dripping umbrella, surrounded by unemployed miners; 'Something must be done. Something shall be done.'? Not – and his mother, so resolute a traditionalist, must have been one of the first to recognise the fact – a remark made by a man prepared to rule on strictly constitutional lines.

People have toyed with the Abdication story from varying angles, but the whole truth remains to be told, years ahead, when the dust has settled.

What is certain is that it must have been a time of great trial for Mary. She wrote of 'the dreadful goodbye. The whole thing was too pathetic for words'.

She had her compensations. She had her other children, and her grand-children, the eldest a pretty child, named Elizabeth but called affectionately Lilibet, who, if she had no brother, would one day be Queen, and whose upbringing must always have regard to that possibility. Mary filled the role of grandmother to perfection, taking Elizabeth and Margaret Rose to Greenwich, to Hampton Court and the Tower of London and other places of historic interest and trying to make the past come alive for them.

She disliked the title of Queen Mother, preferring to be known as Queen Mary, and no doubt remembering how her own mother and mother-in-law had tended to be intrusive, never herself intruded; but she was always there when wanted. She continued her work for many charities, and the beautification of London parks and open spaces by the planting of flowers owes much to her. She had her collections. . . . Would it be lese-majesty to mention her habit of so much admiring, so seeming to covet any item in somebody else's collection that the owner had no choice but to offer it as a gift?

Ageing, but indomitable she went through the Second World War. The son she still thought of as Bertie, but who was known to the world as George VI, persuaded her, somewhat against her will, to leave London and take up residence at Badminton. The other war in which she had played so active a part must have seemed a long way away; as she said, getting old was a bore, but she could set a good example, unruffled, perfectly dressed in her own fashion, calmly doing a crossword puzzle during an air-raid alert.

In 1942 she suffered another bereavement; her youngest son, the Duke of Kent was killed in an aeroplane crash. The news, she said, stunned her, it was unbelievable, but she pulled herself out of her stunned state within a few hours and went to do what could be done to comfort his widow.

In the autumn of 1945, soon after the end of the worst war of all, she saw her lost son again; he came – alone – to visit her. Whether Queen Mary would have received and recognised his wife is debatable – she might have done, but with George VI and his wife so dead set against the Duchess of Windsor, there was nothing that Queen Mary could do.

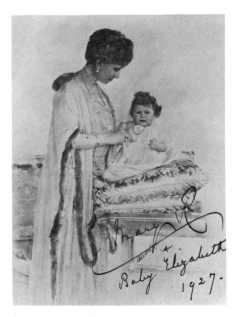

A proud and stately grandmother;
Queen Mary with Lilibet in 1927.

Queen Mary was eighty when Lilibet married Philip; but she was still capable of standing at a reception that lasted from half past nine to a quarter of an hour after midnight. As a wedding present she gave to her grand-daughter the best jewels which she had received at her own wedding.

She lived on to see her great-grandson, Charles, born and christened. As a christening gift she gave him a silver-gilt cup which George III had given to a godson.

She was eighty-four when her second son, George VI died, and she said to a close friend, 'I suppose one must force oneself to go on to the end.' She went straight to Clarence House, saying that Elizabeth's old granny and subject must be the first to kiss her hand. She followed the coffin to West-minster, but did not attend the service or the internment, for although her spirit was indomitable, physically she was feeling her burden of years. She suffered a good deal from sciatica and was sometimes obliged to use a wheel-chair. She retained her mental faculties and her interest in things to the end; a letter written six days before her death was perfectly lucid. It is sad to think that she did not live until the coronation, for although she might not have been able to be present in person, television could have brought all the gorgeous pageantry into her room, and she had shown great interest in all the preparations for the event. However the coronation did not take place until June and Mary died in March, two months before her own birthday.

Elizabeth

Queen to George VI
born 1900, married 1923
See colour plate facing page 176.

The marriage of Albert George, Duke of York to Lady Elizabeth Bowes-Lyon in 1923 was deeply symbolic of a changing world.

There were fewer royal princesses to choose from; and in any case the old idea that a marriage could be of political significance had exploded with the first shot fired in the First World War.

The age of democracy had come; a marriage between a royal duke and a non-royal person – English speaking, though of Scottish blood – was bound to be popular.

And there had been indications that Queen Victoria's far-sighted concern about the results of too much in-breeding had been perfectly valid.

Something, somebody new was needed.

We are told that the Duke of York – Bertie to the family – did his own choosing. And why not? The woman who was later to charm the world could hardly have failed to appeal to a young, painfully shy young man with a stammer. He proposed, and she refused him; why we are not told, but kindly we can be sure. Her mother said that she hoped the Duke of York would find a wife who would make him happy, for he was a man who could be made or marred by his wife. Did the Countess of Strathmore, saying this, give her daughter a straight, significant look?

How much importance should be attached to the well-worn gypsy's prediction about one day wearing a crown? And how much to something even less well-documented? The Prince of Wales is said to have told Elizabeth that she must marry Bertie and would find herself one day at Buckingham Palace.

What we do know is that the Duke of York, despite the physical handicaps which could have been mitigated by a more understanding upbringing, had a good deal of that quality which the eighteenth-century people called

*The relaxed and happy Duke of York and his radiant bride
leave for their honeymoon in 1923.*

bottom, a term of high praise, meaning grit and determination and balance.
He proposed again and was accepted.

In the focus of hind-sight – knowing what lay in store – we should take
pleasure in those honeymoon pictures in which he looks so completely
relaxed and happy. He was twenty-eight, she was twenty-three; Duke and
Duchess of York with a seemingly untroubled future ahead of them.

Charm is as difficult to define as it is impossible to cultivate. Why should
George V, a stickler about time, allow his daughter-in-law to come late to
table and cut short her apologies, 'You are not late, my dear. We must have
sat down two minutes too early'? Why should so many people who have
seen her only in the hurly-burly of a crowd, feel that they have enjoyed a
second's close contact? Blue eyes are not so rare: but these blue eyes focus
and smile and the recipient of that smile feels for half-a-second that he or
she has been recognised as a person. Then it flits on to the next, and the next,
conveying that same tiny bit of magic in a world where magic is in short
supply.

That gift of hers; always at ease, ready with the smile and the right word,
and – except on definitely sad occasions – that appearance of seeming to
enjoy herself even in the dullest of circumstances, was of inestimable value
to a husband who was shy, hesitant of speech and occasionally impatient
with himself for being hesitant. Together they toured South and East Africa,
Australia and New Zealand – all very successfully.

Elizabeth had two children – both girls; not that sex mattered so much;
the Prince of Wales was rising thirty-two when Lilibet was born. Plenty of
time for him to settle down, marry, beget children of his own. But the

incipient threat was there; possibly Queen Victoria would have recognised it; men who doubt their own potency tend to take mistresses of ripe age. Whether or not, behind all *his* charm and beauty and courage the Prince of Wales knew of his secret disability must be a matter of speculation; but all the women with whom his name was ever connected were older than he was, and the woman he eventually married had been married twice before without having a child. Worth, perhaps, a moment's speculation.

The Abdication came in 1936, and in his last speech Edward paid tribute to his sister-in-law; his brother, he said, 'enjoyed one matchless blessing . . . a happy home with his wife and children'.

It was a tricky time both politically and economically; the monarchy could have foundered then. We are told that the man whom a stroke of a pen had made King, broke down absolutely, only too much aware of what the burden, suddenly thrust upon him, meant and under what conditions he must carry it.

When the Duke of York became engaged to Lady Elizabeth Bowes-Lyon genealogists had busied themselves in an attempt to prove that she was of royal lineage. They traced her ancestry back to Robert the Bruce, one of thirteen claimants to the Scots throne. Robert Bruce, who, hiding in a cave, so the stories went, saw a spider weave, and then re-weave her web, and was, by the insect's tenacity, encouraged to try just once more. Both stories may well be true; the new Queen of England could well have been the descendant of the man who watched the spider. What was never in doubt was that there was a great deal of re-weaving to be done.

Nobody could have been better suited for the task. She encouraged as well as supported the King who fought and won a heroic battle against his shyness and his impediment; only those close to him could estimate the strain which those Christmas broadcasts inflicted upon him, and his health suffered. That was one cause for Elizabeth's intransigent attitude towards the Duke of Windsor and his wife. Between them they had imposed upon Bertie.

The Queen continued to be a matchless blessing, always there – exuding serenity – when needed, ready to step back on occasion. And it would be a grave mistake to look upon George VI as a weakling; he had strength of a rare kind – the ability to face his limitations. The Second World War came, and in its darkest days, when Churchill was making his most famous fighting speech, behind the brave words, preparations were going on to set up, in the case of invasion, a provisional government in Canada and to send the royal family to safety there. The King said, '*I* shall stay here'. Naturally his Queen stayed with him and there was one dreadful period during which they must go, almost every day, to visit people whose homes had been reduced to smouldering rubble while they slept – or did not sleep – on the overcrowded platforms of Underground stations. Buckingham Palace was

*Queen Elizabeth's sympathetic smile must have cheered these
Londoners when she and King George VI
visited them after a heavy air-raid.*

bombed and it would not be too wild a guess to say that Elizabeth was *glad*
to say that *her* home had suffered too. Such a view would back up the
personal involvement which no Queen, however much animated by goodwill, had achieved since Elizabeth Tudor died.

The war ended.

It may seem trivial to mention fashion here, but Elizabeth's clothes are
part of the image. As a reaction to the Spartan circumstances of war, so
many women in uniforms and the rest counting their clothes' coupons and
buying, when they could, garments plainly announcing their Utility, there
came a reaction; pretty clothes. And with them Elizabeth stuck. They suited
her; soft, pastel colours, soft fabrics, soft contours. Her clothes are now quite
as individual as Queen Mary's were. She has held to them, through another
change, a period devoted to self-inflicted ugliness, all head-scarves, jeans
and jack-boots; and now – well on into her seventies – she is as pretty as
ever, as refreshing to the eye as a bowl of flowers in a store full of ironmon-
gery. At the same time she manages to convey the impression that if some
emergency happened, demanding the rolling-up of sleeves, hers would be
the first to roll – and they actually did on one occasion, when it came to
rescuing a dog from a drain. Is it permissible to think of her as a marsh-
mallow with a core of good Scotch granite?

George VI, after spells of ill-health, during some of which his Queen
acted as a stand-in, died in 1952, rather unexpectedly, but as peacefully as
he deserved, in his sleep. Overnight, Elizabeth became Queen Mother, free
to retire, to follow her own pursuits and to cultivate interests that range

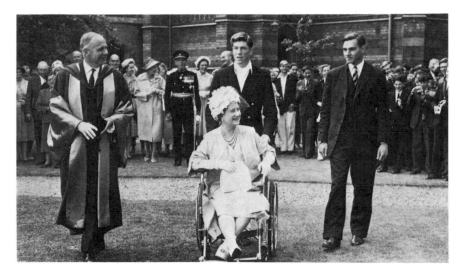

*Charm in a wheel chair; Queen Elizabeth visiting Rugby School,
with a damaged ankle.*

from horse-racing to music, from the collecting of pictures to fishing; but
she was then only fifty-two and of hardy constitution, and she could not be
spared. She still enjoyed an unequalled *personal* popularity. The Queen is
the Queen, traditionally hedged about by the awe and majesty of kings
which no amount of little scampering dogs can quite dispel – it would be
all wrong if they did; the Duke of Edinburgh can be relied upon to be out-
spoken, and occasionally healthily controversial; there are princesses, but
the Queen Mother is the loved one.

It is doubtful if anyone ever uses the term 'Queen Mum' to her face, but
she must know that it is in general currency and she would no more resent
it than Elizabeth Tudor resented being called Good Queen Bess. And it may
be that this special brand of popularity is a two-way traffic affair; she may
draw something from the crowds akin to what she gives; nobody could so
spontaneously stimulate a crowd without being in turn stimulated by it.
And there may lie the clue to her apparent agelessness, a quality shared by
some well-loved actresses. (Didn't Sarah Bernhardt play Juliet when she
was seventy and had a wooden leg?) The Queen Mother has *her* public, and
they know what they want; the prettiness, the ready smile, the serenity and
assurance which can only emanate from a totally un-shy, completely un-
selfconscious person; and while she can stand up she will supply it . . . The
qualification is unnecessary; once when she could not stand up because of a
badly damaged ankle, she had an engagement at a school, and rather than
disappoint the boys, went in a wheel-chair, pushed by the momentarily-
proudest boy in the world. And her radiance shines out, undiminished.

Elizabeth II

Queen in her own right
born 1926, married 1947

See colour plate facing page 177.

Cautious people refuse to discuss any matter which is still *sub judice*; the life-story of anyone now alive and only middle-aged is, at best, little more than half-told. Switches of tense are inevitable and confusing. And there is the future still to come.

The English – and possibly they are not alone in this – like their Queens Regnant to be either touchingly young and pretty, or very old and presumably wise. Elizabeth I and Victoria had qualified on both scores; Mary I, Mary II and Anne had not. Elizabeth II came to the throne when she was twenty-six and pretty, as portraits show. That was an advantage. Another was that she had been trained to the job – quite the most trying one in the world; a job no rational person would envy; a rubber stamp to be applied to other people's decisions, and the everlasting demand for the rubber stamp to be perfect. She is Queen of England, Scotland, Northern Ireland, titular head of many countries which once formed an Empire, but she has no more say in how things should be run than the woman who makes her bed – far less if there is a Bed-Makers' Union and this Bed-Maker is a fully paid up member. The Queen must go, regally clad, to each opening of Parliament and make what is called the Queen's Speech, a concoction of sentiments which vary according to which party is in power; she must receive, with every courtesy, people who are boring, distasteful, even repellent. The wonder is, as Dr Johnson said of a dog dancing, that it is done at all.

But done it is, because from the time when she was ten years old, duty was impressed upon her by her parents and by her grandmother, Queen Mary. And, for the next sixteen years, she had before her her father's example and – but at a different level – her mother's.

It is said that at the age of ten, in that momentous year 1936, she saw Mrs Simpson at a reception and asked, 'Who is she?' Someone could have said,

'She is the woman who will put the crown of England on your head and the burden of being a constitutional monarch on your shoulders.'

Three years later, Princess Elizabeth, hardly out of childhood herself, made a broadcast to all the children of Britain whom the war had made evacuees. Nobody who heard it will ever forget it. Somebody handy with words put the speech together, but *she* delivered it perfectly, in a clear, natural, girlish voice, and with the utmost sincerity.

When we are 'one with Nineveh and Tyre' the second half of the twentieth century will rightly be called the Age of Critics; and to put it into plain words, the critic is one who has failed in his own particular sphere and therefore considers himself qualified to pontificate in every sphere. The Queen of England was an obvious target for such people and one remembers – with rage – how, soon after she became Queen, odious people were criticising her diction.

She was shy to begin with; it was an inherited trait; Queen Mary was shy, so was George VI, and criticism merely inflames the condition. If the Queen, required to make even the briefest formal speech, clutches a bit of paper and seems to read from it, the critics are to blame; that bit of paper is defensive. The Queen is incapable of producing that straight, untroubled look which is her mother's trademark. She looks at the dogs, at the children, or whatever thing is on exhibit.

She was fortunate in finding, quite early, a man she could love, and who would make an acceptable Prince Consort. It is often overlooked that Philip Mountbatten, when he decided to take on British nationality, sacrificed certain rights to the throne of Greece – not of much value at the time – and to the throne of Denmark, which were. He was therefore in a stronger position than Albert had ever been, and a further advantage was that since Elizabeth was not yet a reigning monarch, he was able to propose to her, having gained her father's consent. His British citizenship cost him £10, plus two shillings and sixpence to a Commissioner of Oaths.

It is impossible not to suspect that Prince Albert's ghost walked in the corridors of Prince Philip's mind and had influence on some of his attitudes. He need not have bothered; seldom have two men been more unlike; Philip was popular from the start and has gone on to prove that he is a person in his own right; faced with a crowd he has as much confidence as his mother-in-law. He has wit. Royal speeches may often be pre-prepared, but nobody except the speaker can control the timing and the intonation; in that art Philip is a past master and there is also that pungent astringency which must be his own since it could have no other origin. One is always happily certain that had his destiny led otherwise, he would have been a success – like Elizabeth Tudor, who once said that turned out of England in her petticoat she would make a living.

And surely the finest compliment that Prince Philip could ever receive is that his son, Charles, Prince of Wales imitates him – not consciously – intuitively.

George VI helped. On the day before the wedding he bestowed a number of titles on his prospective son-in-law; only one of them, Duke of Edinburgh, came into general use.

The match was popular with the people, thousands of whom spent the night on the pavements – despite the wedding day being in November – in order to get a good view of the procession. The Princess was calm enough to refuse the sustaining drink offered to her by the King, and afterwards he wrote to her, 'you were so calm and composed during the service and said your words with such conviction that I knew everything was all right'. He had picked out the three qualities which were to go with his daughter along the years; calmness, composure and conviction.

One does not usually associate Queen Mary with the light quip, but when she saw the tablecloth, woven by Gandhi, amongst the plethora of wedding presents, she said that he had sent Elizabeth a loincloth!

A favourite corgi accompanied the couple on their honeymoon. (One thinks of the Empress Josephine's dog, actually on the bridal bed, removed by the great Napoleon, and biting back! One thinks of Queen Victoria, ending one of the most momentous days of her life by bathing her favourite dog.)

By May of the following year, the Princess was pregnant, but, disciplined still, she went with the Duke of Edinburgh to open the Anglo–French Exhibition in Paris; and as any woman who has ever had a baby knows, the first three months are the worst.

(Very, very recently, as a tribute to her fiftieth birthday, a popular magazine interviewed five other *working* women who would be fifty at roughly the same time. Every one of them agreed that she did a good job; and not one of them would have wished to change places with her, the main reason being the lack of privacy, of always being on show.) Of her pregnancy she said, that she might read about it in the papers before she really knew herself.

Later in that summer, symptoms of the King's illness made themselves apparent but it was decided to keep the truth from the Princess until after the baby was born. Prince Charles missed arriving as a first wedding anniversary present by a mere six days. It has been said that the present royal family prefer to think of their Stuart rather than their Tudor ancestry – though one stems from the other. If this is fact, the choice of name is understandable as a gesture, yet puzzling in a woman superstitious enough as never to sit down thirteen at a table, for neither Charles I nor Charles II had a happy story. Still, the Prince has three other names.

Laying the foundation of her reputation as a good family woman, the Princess fed her baby in the natural way for a few months, and then handed him over to expert hands. Up came the critics again! Why not rear her own

*Elizabeth II's first steps on English soil as Queen. A sad, but
historic, moment as she arrived back from her African Tour
where she had been told of her father's death.*

child? The answer was pretty obvious. When her baby was four months
old, her father had his first operation for lung cancer and some of his duties
fell to his daughter; only accredited witches can be in two places at the same
time.

The year 1949 brought her what were probably the happiest and most
carefree days since childhood. The Duke of Edinburgh resumed active
service in the Navy and was stationed at Malta; and like many another naval
wife, the Princess leased a house there and in between necessary official
visits to England – always scrupulously made – lived for a little while, an
almost private life, free of the ever-present press and the TV cameras.

It would be so easy to make a diary of it; the Canadian Tour; the King's
second operation; his brave show of being well again – a day's shooting with
the Duke of Edinburgh on New Year's Day 1952; his seeing his daughter
and her husband off on their African Tour, that tour which was to end at a
place made for tourists, a hotel built into a tree of a size only possible in the
tropics.

News flew fast, even in 1952; somebody told the Duke of Edinburgh that
the King was dead, and Philip broke the news to Elizabeth.

Wearing the black which makes a necessary if unobtrusive part of all
royal luggage, the Queen flew home and walked down the steps of the air-
craft alone to meet her Ministers – and into the pitiless glare of publicity
and the kind of criticism which Americans call nit-picking.

She wasn't trendy enough; she was compared unfavourably with her sister, Margaret Rose and with Jacqueline Kennedy. She refused to send her children – she had two more after Anne – to state comprehensive schools. (She refused to make even the false token gesture of those so-called Left-wingers who send their children to a state comprehensive for one term or two and then move them to Eton.)

She isn't this; she didn't that. What she is and what she has done is too often overlooked. No names, no pack-drill, but the people who stand up in public and ask what purpose does she – and the monarchical system she represents – serve; and does the ordinary tax-payer get his money's worth, should take another look. What she gives is a permanent centre which no President or Prime Minister – or their wives – could possibly provide; she may have no power to change things, but she must be kept informed of all government procedures and is therefore a living repository of yesterday's information which can be drawn upon by 'new boys' who come to office today. She does really *read* the contents of those despatch boxes which have only two keys, one held by the relevant minister and one by her, and since her mind is clear and logical and her memory good, it is advisable – Harold Wilson said so – that anyone before subjecting himself to an official interview with her should do his homework. And one prerogative is still hers – only she can dissolve Parliament and can, if necessary, use delaying tactics which give time for second thoughts and the dying down of hysteria.

It is an unflattering comparison, but she could be said to be that invaluable silent partner who if he does not exist, must be invented. He does not appear in the Board Room, is no longer an executive, but he must be consulted. The last reigning monarch to enjoy complete executive power was Elizabeth Tudor; the last un-royal person to wield it was Cromwell. Parliament took over, inch by inch and eventually handed over the real power to the people – which includes a number who, after eleven years of expensive state education, cannot read. It sounds clumsy and absurd but it works after a fashion; works in fact better than any system so far devised, and that may well be because in the eye of the whirlwind there is this centre of calm.

As to the cost of it, which one Member of Parliament questions, what the Queen takes from public money only just pays for the public state she must keep up – not for her own glorification but in order to flatter the egos of people, many – not all – of very obscure origins. Bring on the horses; the carriages; open the State Apartments at Buckingham Palace, at Windsor; entertain a thousand, two thousand people at a Garden Party. That Member of Parliament should do his homework and remember that costs rise at all levels. It must also be borne in mind that the present royal family are economically aware and, when not on show, live comparatively simple lives. The Queen's great-grandfather, who spent a decade of his life in the twentieth

The Queen, with her husband and youngest son.

century, did not call a dinner a dinner unless it had at least seven courses: his great-granddaughter can make do with three, or two; and if there is a staff shortage, can cook herself.

How Edward VII would shudder to see fields over which he shot at Sandringham full of blackcurrants, to be sold commercially. Thousands of children benefit from the end-product of this enterprise, so palatable, so rich in Vitamin C. What would Henry VIII think of mushroom sheds at Hampton Court, making regular supplies for Covent Garden – or Nine Elms as one must now say?

The Queen's attitude towards Sandringham is symbolic. Edward VII bought it and called it his home in the country; but like many places of the same vintage it was too big and too expensive in upkeep and in staffing to make a home in the late twentieth century, even for a monarch. The Queen considered reducing its size, improving its amenities, and then made a typical decision. Nearby, in that same bit of wind-swept countryside there was another house, small, low-ceilinged; once a rectory, then a doctor's residence, and lately nobody's house. That she bought and restored and made into a family home. Sandringham, which had made tentative attempts to earn its living by admitting visitors to the garden and selling a few pot plants and souvenirs at the gates, will soon be open to the public and will certainly earn its keep, for it will be the first *royal* residence open to all – Hampton Court and Windsor are both State-owned.

So much for purely mundane stuff; the Queen of Great Britain, much as some people would like to cut her down to size and call her 'the tweedy mother of four', still has the mystique of monarchy about her. Something which other countries, either by ill-fortune lost or by bad policy discarded, but still yearn for. Why else should German newspapers, within twenty-four hours of her first visit, say, 'Since yesterday Germany has a Queen; her name is Elizabeth'? Why does she matter to so many people who have either never known or have cast off monarchical rule?

In the beginning, ages away, the monarch was regarded as the one closest in touch with the supernatural world; later he became the best warrior, and then the best diplomat. It may sound somewhat ridiculous now to speak of the Lord's anointed; but there is still something in it. Kings have been beheaded, dethroned, exiled, but look at the track record of those who did the beheading, the dethroning, the exiling . . . it is not good. The political world, like Nature, abhors a vacuum and when something of importance is removed, too many men on the make move in. America threw off George III's yoke and ended with Nixon and Watergate . . . Germany exiled its Emperor and got Hitler . . . Russia killed its Tsar and got the Politburo. One could go on forever, clear down to some temporary ruler of an emergent African state whose wife could find nothing better to do in England than to order a solid gold bedstead.

This country has seen many monarchs, not all of them good, not all of them wise, but all royal and since 1066 all with some claim to be 'of the blood', as the French put it. There was, between 1649 and 1660 a time when there was no King and ambitious men jostled for power, as must happen when no one person has an unquestioned priority. But even Cromwell stopped short at the steps of that empty throne; and when he died, and people were asking 'What next', it was one of Cromwell's own men who came up with the answer, 'restore the monarchy' – revert to the indisputable right. And there is something stabilising about it; the Queen may prefer simple things and a simple life, be happier in a mackintosh and thick shoes walking her dogs in the country than parading in mink in town, but given the occasion, there is never any question of who goes first; she alone has been anointed and crowned. That may sound archaic, but the test of any system must be – does it work? The Queen is living proof that it does. Long may she reign!